# Uninvited Guest

## The Art of Living with Anxiety, Stress, and Overwhelm

By Meagan E. English

Foreword by Koelle Simpson

# Copyright

# Dedication

*To know who you are, what you want, and have
the freedom of heart and mind to pursue it.
This is living.*


For my children, Landon and Gracie, and my
husband, Aaron.
This book is my love letter to you, inspired by you.

# Table of Contents

iv

# Foreword

## by Koelle Simpson

Our cultural narrative has unknowingly shaped such an intense subconscious dialog that we hardly pause to give our highly critical self-talk a second guess. The voice of our inner critic seems to have fully adopted the narrative that each of us must be special, unique, drop-dead gorgeous, highly successful, and exquisitely perfect in all of our endeavors. If we can accomplish this great feat, then we may just be good enough to belong, in the eyes of our society, friends, family, and even with our intimate partners. This ongoing pressure to be good enough has naturally given rise to a life filled with acute anxiety disorders (at worst), or mild, yet incessant, anxiety behaviors (at best).

While she was a student of Equus Coaching™, I had the privilege of witnessing and supporting Meagan English on her personal journey. Meagan seemed to always find a way to embrace her vulnerability and wholeheartedly share with others in her own process toward a deeper level of self-acceptance. When it comes to working alongside highly sensitive horses, who tend to read and broadcast the many nuances in our attempts to hide our own stress and anxiety, there are simply very few places we can actually hide from ourselves.

It was inspiring to watch Meagan release the cultural ideal that she needed to be perfect. Instead she allowed her true nature to be seen and took a more playful, practical approach of implementing the tools that enabled her to transform her own anxiety patterns. This not only caused the horses she regularly worked with to enjoy such a transparent and honest connection with her, but it also enabled Meagan to show up for her clients so that they, too, could feel seen, understood, and truly supported.

*Uninvited Guest: The Art of Living with Anxiety, Stress, and Overwhelm* is a wonderful, clear, down-to-earth approach to help us recognize the various sources of our anxiety, as well as the symptoms of our behavioral coping patterns.

Throughout this book Meagan has thoughtfully shared her own story and the stories of clients (identifying details changed, of course), in order to guide us on a journey that enables each of us to witness that we are not alone with our anxious inner dialog. She offers simple and effective tools that pave the way for embracing our anxiety and living a more peaceful and authentic life.

I hope you will enjoy this genuine and insightful read as much as I did.

Koelle Simpson

Founder of the Koelle Institute for Equus Coaching

www.KoelleInstitute.com

# Bonus Chapter: Finally, Freedom!

## Download and read this first!

Dear Reader—

–I'm so happy to have you join me on this journey. My book is meant to show you that you're not alone and to start teaching you basic tools that can help you learn to live more fully, freely, and peacefully alongside your own uninvited guest, whatever form it may take: Anxiety. Stress. Overwhelm. And all of the sources and symptoms that come along with it.

**Read the Bonus Chapter first——download it now by visiting**
www.meaganenglishcoaching.com/uninvitedguest/bonus

# Introduction

*"Living with anxiety is like being followed by a voice. It knows all your insecurities and uses them against you. It gets to the point when it's the loudest voice in the room. The only one you can hear."*
~Author unknown

## Anxiety, by Any Other Name

If you're here, you probably know this: anxiety, in all its shapes and sizes, can wreak havoc on our lives. There are many types of anxiety disorders. The gut-wrenching pain of a panic disorder. The traumatic panic of post-traumatic stress disorder (PTSD). The constant devil-on-your shoulder feeling of Obsessive-Compulsive Disorder. There's also the subtle (to outsiders) anxiety that affects high-achieving and seemingly unaffected people all over the world. I know. I've been living with some of these uninvited guests my whole life.

If what you are feeling is any of the above, and if it is simply (and also not simply) nagging worry, constant concern, overwhelm paralysis, a tendency toward perfectionism, and an inability to know what you want and say what you feel, I have to tell you: I feel you. I've been there. Sometimes I pop back in for a visit.

1

And this book is for all of you.[1]

You may recognize yourself in the questions that run through your mind…an anxious mind…that nagging (and atrociously annoying) little voice that is constantly second-guessing you:

*"What if I make a huge mistake on this project and get fired?"*

*"If I apply for this promotion and then fail, everyone will know I'm a fraud."*

*"I'm just not that smart——eventually someone's going to figure it out."*

*"I would never want to disappoint my boss——I don't think she likes me very much as it is."*

*"I can't really say no to anyone——the reason they value me as an employee is that I always say yes."*

*"Yeah, I don't really like my job, but I don't think I could actually be successful at anything else."*

Here's what I know: My form of anxiety may look very different from yours. It looks different from my son's. It's different from my daughter's. It's different from my client, Fisher's. Different doesn't mean better

---

[1] Let me say here that if you're suffering from an anxiety disorder that is so debilitating that you cannot safely function, this may not be the book for you—— but there are many qualified professionals in the world who would love to support you.

or worse, more difficult or easier. Different does, however, mean that it's even more important for you to be able to recognize what's happening in your mind, your body, and, subsequently, your behavior so that you can put a name to it and figure out how to live with it. Through it, even.

For example, my daughter has social anxiety—Before practicing with her team for a new season or going to the first day of school, she literally makes herself sick with worry. I've seen tears, vomit, hyperventilation. Her stomach is always affected, and her heart rate skyrockets. Now, mind you, this isn't a new team or a new school. No—it's just been a little bit of time between gatherings. In her behaviors, the symptom of her anxiety comes out distinctly as people-pleasing. Performance anxiety. And perfectionism? Perfectionism is both a source of and a symptom of her anxiety that is interwoven through everything she does. It is the armor she wears to avoid feeling even more anxious, the pressure of which sometimes actually makes her feel more anxious.

My son, on the other hand, suffers from both generalized and separation anxiety (yes – clinically diagnosed). His symptoms come in the form of tics——actually diagnosed as Tourette Syndrome. It's mild, but it's there. He doesn't make himself sick to his stomach like my daughter does. And yet, just by glancing at him, I can tell what his anxiety is doing. If he's still and even-keeled, he's calm. The more movement, the more anxiety. My son's not a perfectionist——and he's definitely not a people-pleaser. Fear of judgement, fear of failure, and "what if" syndrome are the primary sources of his anxiety, and through anxiety, his symptoms show up as procrastination, an unwillingness to make decisions, and a lack of confidence.

I have the distinct pleasure of knowing that I may have gifted these traits to my children. Over the years I've been diagnosed with mild depression, Obsessive-Compulsive Disorder, Trichotillomania——but never 'simply' anxiety. What I've learned, though, is that those diagnoses are the results of the anxiety that I'm feeling and have never put a name to. Big project due? Great——I'm going to reorganize the closet! Critical meeting in two days? Sweet——I'm just going to pull out some eyelashes! New job offer? I'm just going to need to crawl under my covers for a nice long nap before I turn it down (just in case they really don't want me anyway).

Ironically, I've never told anyone I was anxious. Nervous? Yes. Stressed? To the max. Agitated? Absolutely. Frenetic? Always. Anxious? Nah. Not really. Why not? Because it feels hard to explain. Because there is a stigma to saying "I'm anxious" that can feel like a weakness. What I struggle with on the inside doesn't really look like what I thought anxiety was on the outside. At the culmination of my career, I made a solid six-figure income, flew around to meetings on a private jet, supervised an average of fifteen direct reports at a time with a portfolio including thirteen business entities, nearly a thousand staff members, and around five million dollars in net profit on an annual basis.

*For God's sake, does that sound like someone with anxiety to you?*

It does to me—now. What you see on my outside doesn't reflect what I feel on my inside. And inside I felt anxious all the time. Throughout this book you'll hear many more stories of real clients with whom I have worked——beautiful, successful, smart, engaging, funny, accomplished people——who knew something was holding them back but simply couldn't put a name to it.

- Zoe came to me because she wanted a promotion and to make more money, but she felt afraid to try anything because of her tendency toward perfectionism.
- Barrett wanted to succeed in his promotion and be happy in his work, but he was distracted by constantly wondering if people thought he was doing a decent job.

- Sandra wanted to make a decision about which path to take her career in but didn't trust herself.
- Michelle was overwhelmed: she made more than three hundred thousand dollars annually, was a VP, had a new baby, and two side jobs that she couldn't drop because people might think she'd failed.
- Fisher had been with the same company and in the same position for eight years and still couldn't figure out how to prioritize his work, which kept him stuck and not moving forward.
- Maddie was entering her junior year of high school and struggling with the confidence to make decisions about college and earn the coveted spot on the varsity volleyball team.
- Nora had received two promotions in less than a year and was being placed at the head of a department in which she was the newest member, and she wasn't sure she could do it.
- Evie was a successful midlevel manager with a six-figure income who was debilitated by shyness and insecurity and wanted to be considered for a promotion.

Here's what they had in common:

An underlying anxious feeling that manifested in the form of perfectionism through and through. And also? Procrastination.. Overwhelm paralysis. Overcommitment (and sheer busyness). Fear of failure. Fear of judgement. Self-judgement. Lack of confidence (regardless of their apparent successes). Ultimately, they felt stuck. Unsure of what to do, where to turn, what direction to take. What they found——*what we found*——was freedom.

We found the freedom to realize our desires and dreams. The freedom to make mistakes. The freedom to ask for what we want and risk rejection and acceptance in the process. The freedom to take big risks, survive big failures, and receive big rewards. The freedom to try new things. The freedom to step outside of our comfort zones.

*The freedom to be who we are.*

In the following chapters I'll share some of the tools and techniques that I've used not only for myself, but with my children, my friends, and my clients. My deepest hope is that you'll read this book, recognize yourself in some of the stories, and take something away that can help you move forward with the career and life that will feel happy, fulfilling, and free. You'll see stories of the clients who have not only changed themselves, but the stories of the clients who have changed me. Anxiety, in all its guises and all its costumes, can feel isolating.

You're not alone.

Read along, lets explore the sources, symptoms, and behaviors that are associated with anxiety, stress and overwhelm together.

# Chapter 1: Silent but Deadly

*"The biggest barrier to self-compassion is perfectionism. Cultivating self-compassion is a practice. First we must let go of the idea that perfectionism will keep us safe."*
*~Brené Brown*

## Perfectionist Problems (source/symptom)

Has anyone ever said to you: "Wow! You're so perfect!" or "My goodness, is there anything you *can't* do?" In all honesty, I'd always believed that perfectionism was something to aspire to. Something that would make me great——better than everyone else. Desirable. Unbeatable. Popular. Loved. Beloved. And hey——it's possible that those things may have happened had I achieved perfection.

There's just one little problem: perfection isn't real. It's not a thing you can achieve. So what was really happening for me when I was striving for perfection? I just kept trying to attain something that was unattainable…time and time again. And I'll give you a hint: it didn't feel very good. It felt like failure.

Because perfection was something that I could work for and work for and work for and never ever achieve.

Time and time again I've had perfection-aspiring clients say to me, "Well, what's wrong with trying? What's wrong with working hard? What's wrong with wanting to be great?" My answer is always, "Absolutely nothing."

There's nothing wrong with working hard. Hoping for better. Aiming to achieve more than you did the moment before. But here's the kicker: you can do all of those things and never actually reach that goal. The perfect job. The perfect marriage. The perfect book. Or, you actually *can* reach your goal and *still* not feel good enough. Because the problem with perfectionism—one of the many problems with perfectionism—is that it is unattainable. Unachievable. And guess what? If you're a perfectionist, then all of that "failure" to reach your goal doesn't inspire you—it makes you feel even more imperfect than you actually are.

There. I said it. You're imperfect.

I'm really sorry. It took me a good thirty-five years to hear that without going into a near panic attack.

I'll let you in on a sweet, sweet secret: once I accepted imperfect and realized that I could lower that lofty goal from "being perfect" to "being me," I felt delicious, glorious freedom.

Why? Perfectionism, for me, came out as an intense desire to avoid criticism. And in order to avoid criticism, I had to make sure I didn't do anything that I didn't know how to do. In order to avoid doing what I didn't know how to do, I had to make sure I never tried anything new. And when I never tried anything new, guess what happened?

Nothing.

Absolutely nothing happened.

Seriously, I was stuck in the most boring, ridiculous, perfectly manicured life. And it was stifling.

Perfectionism is a bit like a cold. It's subtle. It's annoying. Lots of people have it, and it shows up differently for just about everyone. There's no quick fix. Those damn colds come around over and over again with no warning. Have you ever had kids in day care? When they're tiny and their immune system is being built up, they get colds all the time——they bring them home to you, and you get them too. Over time, they still catch colds, but it happens less and less often, and the colds are less and less intense. That's how I feel about learning to live with anxiety-instilled perfectionism. It may always be there——we're not

11

going to cure you with this one book, after all——but just like your immune system becomes strengthened against the common cold, your brain and your heart will become stronger in learning how to live with perfectionist tendencies.

Perfectionism, for me, is unique, as it relates to anxiety, stress, and overwhelm. It is both a source of anxiety and a symptom of anxiety——it runs (seemingly innocuously) throughout each of the client files you'll read through. Perfectionism is a source of anxiety because we strive for it——over and over—— to no avail. It also shows up as a symptom of anxiety— —we feel anxious and believe that if only we can be perfect, that will help us feel some relief. It's a part of why this can be so difficult—because it happens in spirals: "If I'm practically perfect, I'll feel less anxious, and the more anxious I feel, the more perfect I have to be." Man, do I know this circle well. I live it every day. My daughter does. My clients do, too. Zoe's story is a perfect example of how perfectionism shows up as both source and a symptom of anxiety:

When I first started working with my client Zoe, she was recently married, had just purchased a new home, and was in a stable job with a great company. She had been an executive assistant for the past six years and was feeling a little bored. She had her eyes on a promotion to a department management position and had been told she still needed to work through a few specific challenges before she was considered for the promotion. When she called me, she told me that she was generally happy in her job, but she wanted a new challenge and to make more money.

"What is it that you're hoping to gain through our work together?" I'd asked.

Zoe was able to list several things that she hoped I could help her with. "I'm never quite satisfied with what I have," she told me. "I want to do more and be more. I also know that I need help with managing my stress level, with how I relate to people, and how I manage my time. I get nervous in meetings with superiors because I'm afraid I'll say or do something wrong, and when anyone else questions my work, I get very defensive. I just can't handle their criticism. As if *they're* perfect."

Right away I noticed a theme: a desire to appear flawless.

"Zoe," I said. "Say a little bit more about what happens when someone questions your work."

"Well,—I'll give you an example. I've been working for months on creating a corporate compliance program. I researched it, wrote it, and developed it. And just last week, Steven——a new guy to the company——started asking me questions about it. And not only that——he started asking other people questions about it! None of it is any of his business!"

"Why did it bother you that Steven was asking questions about the corporate compliance program?"

"Because he was implying that I missed something! That I didn't do it right!"

"Did he say to you or to anyone else that you missed something or didn't do it right? I'm just curious."

"Of course not——but I can tell that's what he meant. He was treating me like I'd messed it up somehow," Zoe said.

As we talked further, it became clear that Zoe's challenges with fielding questions from her peers, speaking up in meetings with her supervisors, and how she managed her time were all stemming from one common theme: a burning desire not to mess up in the slightest. A need to be perceived as unflappable, better than others, and someone who does not mess up. Ever. Perfectionism. At its finest.

In the workplace, specifically, perfectionism that stems from anxiety (diagnosed or not) can become a major hindrance in forward momentum. An inability to take criticism from a peer can look like an inability to get along with others. A reluctance to speak up in a meeting with your supervisor can appear to be a lack of initiative. And a hesitancy to create or sustain forward momentum in projects due to a desire to know exactly how to do it before you start? A time management issue.

In Zoe's case, these were all excellent opportunities to get clear on the underlying issue ("It just needs to be done perfectly the first time") as a product of perfectionism, which had arisen from a worry that being less than perfect would hold her back from excelling in her career,—and voilà! We created an opportunity to move forward.

Once Zoe realized that her desire to be perfect was actually the thing that was throwing up all her obstacles, we dove in. And where did we start? Vulnerability.

A few sessions later, Zoe and I again revisited her burning desire to punch her coworker Steven right in the throat. "Do you absolutely, without a doubt, unequivocally know that it's true that Steven thinks that you handled the research, creation, and roll-out of the corporate compliance policy wrong?" I asked.

"Yes! I know that's what's going on!"

"Did you ask him that?"

After a long and awkward pause, Zoe said, "Well...no."

"Why not?"

"Because…I don't want him to think I care. And I don't want him to think I'm worried."

"Zoe, let me switch gears for a minute. Let's say that you went home from work last night, forgot to let the cats out, and they peed all over your brand-new couch. And your husband was pissed at you. In his mind, you just didn't give a shit about that couch. You didn't care about how much money you had both worked and saved to buy the couch. You were being disrespectful, and, in fact, you probably wanted the cat to piss all over his favorite spot on that godforsaken couch. Now, *you* know that's not true, but he actually believes all of this, and as he fumes over it, he's getting madder and madder. Until he's just about to blow. You can tell something's wrong, but he won't talk to you about it. In this scenario, would you want him to keep fuming or buck up and ask you why you did it?"

Laughing, Zoe said, "Well, of course I'd want him to ask me! And if he didn't, I'd think he was a big wimp and super immature!"

"Ah. Interesting. So…is it fair to say that if he got the nerve to ask you why you let the cat piss all over the couch that you might not think he was a wimp, and you might appreciate that he actually cared enough to start a conversation?"

"Mmmm…yes."

16

"Is it possible, then, that you asking Steven why he's questioning you and if he's concerned that you made a mistake might be a relief to both of you?"

Zoe rolled her eyes and sighed. "*Ugh.* Meagan! Why do you do this to me? Yes!"

"What happens if you discover that he actually does think that you did something wrong?"

"I'll be humiliated."

"Why will you feel humiliated?"

"Because I made a mistake."

"And what's so bad about making a mistake?"

"Oh...well..." Zoe said. "I guess that I just want it to be perfect."

"Is it possible that everything can be perfect all the time?"

"Well...no. Of course not...but...it feels so awful to think about it not being perfect and even more awful to think that someone else might know it's not perfect."

"So what we're really talking about here is vulnerability. Brené Brown says that what feels like weakness to me looks like courage to someone else. Does that sound true to you?" I asked.

17

"Huh. I guess it does. So what you're saying is that I might feel like a weenie if I ask Steven what he thinks of the work that I did, but to him I might look like someone who's strong and is confident in my work and is even willing to be okay with making a mistake and then learning from it?"

"I'm saying I think that's very possible. What do you think?"

"I like it. Thinking about it that way makes me feel like I can have a conversation with him and remember that what I'm doing is a reflection of bravery——not a sign of weakness."

"Excellent. What do you want to do relative to Steven, then?"

"I'm going to ask to sit down and talk to him tomorrow. Instead of beating myself up over things that…well…frankly might not even be true…I'd rather get to the bottom of what's going on. And maybe I'll still be beating myself up, but at least it will be over something real!" said Zoe, finally laughing.

Vulnerability. I do believe that the willingness to be vulnerable—to be seen, to be accepted or rejected—can actually build our confidence muscle (we'll come back to that later). Vulnerability may actually be the antidote to perfectionism. A willingness to not only be seen, but to be seen in a reality that isn't perfect, can start to heal perfectionist tendencies, and reduce them to niggling thoughts instead of a way of life.

A former coach and dear friend once asked me what I grew up believing that vulnerability was: "Weakness," I'd said. "A chink in the armor where the soft parts are exposed and danger is imminent. It's scary, threatening. Vulnerability means that I'm unprotected."

Now, however, I watch my children practice and embrace vulnerability. My son's teacher asked him if she could talk with his class about his Tourette's—what it is, what it means, how it affects him. He stared at her for a moment. He said yes. I remember that in that moment I could not have been prouder. For him, that "yes" may have felt like weakness—like being exposed. But when he said yes, all I saw was a brave and strong young man standing in front of me. Weak? Never.

So how does vulnerability reduce perfectionism?

It forces us to accept and reveal that we are not perfect. That we make mistakes. That sometimes we make the wrong decisions, and when we can be vulnerable at those times, we start healing our tendency toward perfectionism. We see that even when we say or do the wrong things, when we are vulnerable and open, we can still be accepted and loved. When we embrace perfectionism, however, we tend to hide: We hide from rejection. We hide from judgement. We hide from all of it. And we try so hard to protect the places that our armor doesn't cover that sometimes we forget to fight for the life that we want at all.

In the workplace, when we're facing a situation, we can choose one or the other: Do I want to be vulnerable and try something? Or do I want to try to appear perfect and play it safe?

When you are willing to be vulnerable, you begin to embrace an implicit acknowledgement that you aren't perfect, and you might start on a project only to realize that it's going to cost half a million more dollars to complete then you'd originally thought.

Guess what? You started the project. Now you know. Good job. And *what if,* instead of starting the project, you actually create something that has never before been realized, and make your company more money than they know what to do with? Had you never started the project, you'd never have known. Perfectionism can hold you back—vulnerability can give you wings.

When you're willing to be vulnerable and ask someone what they think about you as a leader, you might hear that you're a little "holier than thou." That maybe you could talk less and listen more. Guess what? Now you get to become a better leader. High five. And *what if,* instead, you hear that your willingness as a leader to be open, try new things, and take feedback inspired that employee to go back to school and provide a better life for their family? Had you never asked, you yourself never would have been inspired in turn. Perfectionism can push you down—vulnerability can teach you to fly.

When you're willing to speak up in a meeting and share with your boss that you think a different strategy could be more efficient, you may be told, "Hey, thanks for your opinion, but we're going to do it this way this time." Guess what? Now they know that you're paying attention. They know that you care. That you have an opinion that could help them. 'Atta kid. What if you had never spoken up because you didn't want to say the wrong thing? Perfectionism can teach you to hide—vulnerability can allow you to show up.

Being vulnerable doesn't mean that you're never wrong and that you'll never get torn down. You will. It happens to all of us.

But you——the real you——is showing up. You are moving! You're figuring things out——going somewhere——learning something——creating a richer, more meaningful life. You're living bravely. (And hey, if you've never read Brené Brown's book, *Daring Greatly*, I highly recommend it——that is what you're going to do when you embrace vulnerability and start using it as the antidote to perfectionism! You will dare. Greatly.)

The reality, my friend, is that when we are trying not to get anything wrong, we're not doing anything at all. Perfectionism is both a source and a symptom of anxiety——it's the fear of being judged and the fear of failure. I hear it all the time, and I say it even more: perfect is the enemy of done. Perfect is the enemy of good.—Perfect can even be the enemy of great. Perfectionism is procrastination. That's why we start here.

Perfectionism causes us to hide. We don't want to be vulnerable because it exposes our imperfections.— When we hide, we hide those soft spots, those places that it may hurt to show that we're all just really perfectly imperfect humans.

When we can let go of that desire to appear perfect, it allows us to take risks. Try new things. Learn. Grow. Live. Repeat.

When Zoe finally did reach out to Steven, she discovered that the idea that she had screwed something up had never actually entered his mind—he simply didn't understand the program.—He wanted to learn from her, to find out why she made the decisions she'd made, and to further his own understanding. When Zoe asked Steven his thoughts on her work, she didn't discover that he was out to get her. Instead, she discovered that she could be the leader he was looking for all along. She broke down that wall of desired perfectionism and came out the other side stronger, more confident, and more capable.

Freedom. She found freedom not only from what she thought was his judgement, but more importantly, from her own.

Think about it:

What are you trying to do perfectly today? What are you trying to avoid screwing up at work? Is aiming to be the perfect employee working for you? Are you inspired? Energetic? Moving forward?

Is aiming to be the perfect parent helping you to enjoy the journey of parenting? Or is it causing you stress, worry, and anxiety? (I think I might have to write my next book about parenting!)

Is aiming to be the perfect wife and friend helping you to slow down, enjoy the moments you have, live in the present, and participate in hobbies and activities that make you laugh until your gut aches?

Is there anything that you can give yourself permission to do right now that might make any of the above better? What can you try that's new? Yes, it might make you feel a little anxious, but if you can give yourself permission to do it totally imperfectly, it might even make you feel a little alive.

In order to move away from perfectionism to show up more fully and authentically in your work and life, consider giving yourself permission to do something at work, at home, or even on your own completely imperfectly, and see if it changes you and how you feel.

This is an exercise that I use with clients regularly, and it's very simple and very powerful (if you're willing to do it).

For the next seven days, write yourself a permission slip each day and put it somewhere you'll see it regularly. Date it. Write down, "I give myself permission to…"

…go to a Zumba class even if I feel completely foolish.

…ask my boss if there are any upcoming projects I can take the lead on.

…invite the new guy at work out for lunch.

…Fill in the blank.

It doesn't need to be something big——but it should be something you've been avoiding because you don't know how to do it or you just want it to be perfect.—Now consider flexing that vulnerability muscle and treating your anxiety-induced perfectionism by doing it anyway.

Just try it. Once. For me.

I guarantee that, if nothing else, you'll see that you will survive.

And man, is that freeing.

# Chapter 2:
# Procrastination
# Predicaments

*"The best way to get something done is to begin."*
*~ Author Unknown*

## Procrastination (source/symptom)

In my first couple of sessions with my client, Barrett, a project manager for a large company, we spent a lot of time talking about his childhood. He had grown up in a household with a dad who was never completely satisfied, and a Grandpa who was downright mean. At the end of the first session, Barrett confided in me that he had a hard time letting go of control in any project because he wanted to make sure he had all his bases covered—t's crossed, i's dotted and several other metaphors for being 100 percent thorough and detail-oriented. Barrett's "thoroughness" was even keeping him from tackling a home A/C installation.

"Barrett, help me understand why you feel like you have to cover that level of detail on every single project—including installing the AC in your own attic?"

"Well, because I just don't want to be questioned later and not have thought it through."

"So let's talk about this AC unit," I prodded. "Who might question you about it? It's in the attic, right? Do people go into your attic very often?"

"No," he admitted. "But someone could. I wouldn't want my wife to ask me why I installed it and didn't paint the trim."

"Why not?"

"Because I would get pissed. I wouldn't like that she's questioning me about that."

"So imagine that your wife walks up to you and says, 'Barrett, I was just in the attic—why didn't you paint the trim around the AC unit?' Tell me the first thought that enters your head."

"Really? Well…the first thought that would enter my head is 'What the fuck?'" Barrett answered, laughing (and blushing).

"Okay. Perfect," I said. "'What the fuck?' Why do you think 'What the fuck?' Be completely honest."

"Because I know she's judging me."

"She's judging you? How do you know?"

Barrett became teary. "Because I should have painted the fucking trim when I did it!"

"So she's judging you for not painting the trim, and now your work and all that time installing the AC unit means nothing. Okay. Let me ask you this: why haven't you installed the AC unit yet? Do you know?"

Barrett started really crying. "Because I haven't had time to think it all through. Maybe I'm lazy! I don't know! I need to have all of the equipment, I need to know what color of trim matches the wall, I have to go to the store, and I need time to figure it all out. If I don't have it all figured out then I can't start, and I can't get it all figured out because I don't know where to start!"

At this point I started to laugh (it's okay—Barrett doesn't take me too seriously—I only work with clients who can laugh with me). "Barrett!" I scold. "It is going to be 100 degrees this week! Are you kidding me right now? Do you think your wife is going to be more pissed because the trim isn't painted or because she's having a heat stroke in the sweltering living room?!"

Barrett was abashed and started to laugh with me. "Okay, okay, okay…you have a point. So now what?"

"To use your own words, 'What the fuck?!' Just go buy the AC unit and figure the rest out later!"

29

I'm happy to report that it wasn't laziness or unwillingness to install the AC unit—in fact, it got installed that very next weekend—without the appropriate trim painted until a much later date. And guess what? His wife didn't care.

This specific situation may sound silly to those of you sitting at home. I get it. And I'm wondering if you can see what was happening here: anxiety-fueled procrastination. The fear and worry that the project may not turn out right, the anxiety over knowing where to start and wondering how to figure it all out, showing up in the simple but overwhelming behavior of just not doing it at all.

I bet you've been here before. Any of these situations sound familiar?

*My client Fisher: "I need to clean up my office." Me: "Well why haven't you done it yet?" Fisher: "Because there's so much to do!" Me: "Well what's the first thing you need to do?" Fisher: "Everything!" Me: "That's why you haven't started. Your goal is too big."*

*My client Elena: "I need to organize my emails." Me: "Why haven't you done it yet?" Elena: "Because I don't know where to start." Me: "Well what's the first thing you need to do?" Elena: "I don't know! To get it all done right, it's going to take hours, and I don't have that kind of time!" Me: "Ah. Well that's why you haven't started yet. Your goal is too big, and you're not willing to let it be messy while you figure it out."*

*My client Emily: "I'd like to set up a marketing system." Me: "Why haven't you done it yet?" Emily: "Because I want to make sure I do it all correctly the first time, and I'm not sure where to begin because I've never done it before. I don't want to make a mistake." Me: "I see. Well that's why you haven't started yet. Fear of doing it wrong."*

Do you notice a theme here? If not, let me clue you in: all of these people, including Barrett, want to do *the whole job perfectly the first time*, and that pressure is keeping them from figuring out how to begin at all—let alone finish! Procrastination is a by-product of anxiety-produced perfectionism…causing even more stress, confusion, and anxiety. Man, have I been here before!

Let me first say that not one of these people is lazy, stupid, or unmotivated—Not one! Every single client I work with is smart, capable, and hardworking—In fact, if they didn't want to work hard, they wouldn't put so much pressure on themselves to do it right.

This kind of procrastination is not a personality flaw, it's a symptom—a side effect of a much deeper problem (yes…you named it: anxiety). You want to complete something big and awesome? It becomes too big and awesome to start. You want to impress and amaze with your end product? It becomes too much pressure to begin.

Again, perfect is the enemy of done, my friend. You want it done? Start it! What's the first small step that you can take? Break it down! If you want it perfect, wait for someone else to do it (and then be annoyed because *it can't be perfect*!)

It's a fantastic thing to be able to see the forest for the trees... Seeing the end result and the big picture are important when it comes to strategy and vision—these are signs of a great leader. However, to build a forest, first you need to plant the tree.

With my clients, I like to say, "Hold the vision. But hold it *lightly*. Let it be there to guide you, but allow it to change if it wants to." The vision is the inspiration— it's the end goal. But to get there, baby steps must be taken. In all of the cases above, my clients needed to start building the forest by planting a tree without worrying if a drought was on its way. Only then could they finally see the forest they envisioned begin to take shape.

A couple sessions later, Barrett and I were working together again. We'd spent much of the previous sessions learning to notice when he was reacting with a "what the fuck" response (everyone's is different, but that was definitely his!), and then starting to take small risks in order to take a few steps forward.

"So Barrett, what's on your mind today that you'd like some support with?" I began.

"Well... I've been given a really big project. I'm excited about it because it gets me out into the field with the executives, and I can get really creative with some of the solutions in more challenging business units. This could really help me build my portfolio so that I can be ready for the next promotion that's offered in the engineering department!"

"Great! Congratulations! So how's the project going?"

"Oh. Well...that's where you come in. I haven't actually done anything on it yet."

"When was this project assigned?"

"About a month ago."

"Sounds like we should come up with a strategy. But first, why haven't you started?"

Barrett shook his head. "I know why I haven't started. Because I want to make sure that when I go into the field, I have everything figured out, and no one will tell me that my idea won't work. I know. I know. We've talked about this before."

I laughed. "Okay, good. At least you know what's stopping you. Now it's time to get started. Why would it be bad if someone tells you, 'No, that idea won't work at this location.'?"

"Because then I'll feel like I've failed to complete the project for them timely."

"Barrett. You know I have to ask this. Are you completing the project timely for them now?"

"Oh. My. God. No. I'm just waiting to do it so I don't do it wrong so that they won't feel like I'm not doing it, and in turn, I'm not doing it! Holy shit!"

"I don't quite know what you just said, but I think you might have just had a lightbulb moment there. Good! So… Now it's time to break this sucker down. Let's talk about baby steps," I said.

With clients who suffer from what I call "overwhelm paralysis" (or the big picture stopping them in their tracks) I like to use a very simple tool (notice I didn't say easy!). Overwhelm paralysis is simply one form of serious procrastination that comes by way of anxiety (the thing to do is too much, too big, or too overwhelming, and I don't know where to start, I'm too nervous to start, I have no idea what I'm going to do, etc.):

The tool? Baby steps. The method here is to keep asking, "What do I need to do first?" and "What do I need to do before that?" then "What do I need to do before that?" until you get to the first, little, teeniest, tiniest baby step that is so small and easy it would be ludicrous not to take it.

Here's a very simplistic example:

"I want to get this dish into the dishwasher."

"What do you need to do first?"

"I need to open the dishwasher."

"What do you need to do before that?"

"I need to walk to the dishwasher."

"What do you need to do before that?"

"I need to rinse my dish."

"What do you need to do before that?"

"I need to scrape the scraps into the trash."

"What do you need to do before that?"

"Walk to the trash can."

"What do you need to do before that?"

"I need to stand up from the table."

"Good. Now you can start."

Sounds silly, right? The truth is that most people (including myself) who tend to suffer with anxiety in the workplace (or anywhere, for that matter), suffer with the by-products and symptoms of perfectionism and procrastination. We tend to be so focused on how to get things done so that we can prove ourselves and not be stressed that we become really stressed and can't get anything done!

In addition to the "baby step" tool above, I also love to introduce my clients to two additional concepts that can help them when they're feeling stalled by overwhelm paralysis and procrastination.

The first concept that I (alongside my clients) use is "the 3 T's" (adapted from my mentor Martha Beck's "3 B's"). The aim of this tool is to really start taking a look at what actually needs to stay on your "to-do" list and what can come off. In order to really learn how to live more freely alongside your anxiety (by reducing stress and overwhelm), it's imperative to start learning how to subtract things from your life that don't actually serve you. And from there? You learn how to make the things that you choose to keep in your life (and on your to-do list) a little bit more enjoyable. Here are the "3 T's" and how they work.

**Trash It**: Is something on your "to-do" list that doesn't actually need to be there? Can you trash it and no one will be the wiser? For me, "Trash It" items tend to be things like baking cookies for a playdate or folding my underwear before I put them away. "Trash

It" items at work sometimes come down to what I actually have time for. Yes, I'd love to send out birthday cards to every friend and client that I have, but then I'd be writing birthday cards for an hour every day. I mean, sure, it'd be nice, but is it *necessary*? My answer is almost always a resounding no.

**Trade It**: Is there something on your "to-do" list that you aren't really that good at or also don't like? Is there something else you'd much rather be doing? Is there someone in your life with whom you could trade tasks and make both of your task lists not only more enjoyable but feel more manageable? In my world, I often trade tasks with my husband. He would much prefer to make dinner, and I would much prefer to shuttle the kids. Trade. For work I love to plan logistics, market, and organize timelines for workshops and events—my friend, who also has her own business, is far better at designing landing pages for registration and writing the marketing and website content. Perfect trade, as far as I'm concerned! Hate accounting but love marketing? See if you can partner up with a peer or coworker and help each other out. Hate Excel but love WordPress? Find someone to trade "to-dos" with. You may not be able to get out of some things (they may have to live in your life and on your to-do list) but you can get creative with how you get it done so that you at least enjoy the task you're given.

**Tune It Up**: In reality, these are tasks that you can neither trash nor trade, so you have to tune it up somehow to make it more enjoyable. (My mentor, Martha Beck, calls this one "Bettering It.") I'm an entrepreneur, and I run my coaching and speaking practice as a small business. That means sometimes I have to do the accounting—blech. I hate accounting. I could hire someone, but I'm not really inspired to do that. So instead, I "tune it up." When I know I'm setting aside time to do my accounting, I invite other entrepreneur friends over to do theirs with me—we sit at the dining room table, sipping hot coffee and sharing stories—occasionally we get distracted by a good joke or a belly laugh. And then we're back to the accounting. I tune it up so that I can stay accountable to the task I have ahead of me, and I end up really enjoying it too. In my corporate life, if I had to put together a compliance report or review financial statements, I tried to sit down and do it alongside my counterpart, or sit in a Starbucks with a pumpkin spice latte. There are lots of ways to tune up your task list— ultimately anything that can help you improve your perception and reduce your anxiety about doing the task can be used as a "tune-up" tool.

The final tool that I use on a regular basis with my clients is simply a conversation about values and priorities. Your values exist, whether you spend time thinking about and acknowledging them or not. Your values are the things that are most important in your work and life. Your priorities are different from your values, but (ideally) should be designed around them.

Let me give you an example of what I mean. If quality time with your family is high on your list of values but you're working sixty hours a week, your values and priorities may not be in alignment. Alternately, if you value financial freedom but are considering changing careers entirely (and perhaps starting in an entry level position), your values and priorities may also not be aligned.

In Barrett's case, and in many others, I have found that using these tools with my clients helps them not only to shift from procrastination into forward momentum, but in turn, helps to move through (and therefore alleviate) anxiety. When procrastination holds us back, we tend to wonder what's wrong with us, in effect increasing our stress and anxiety. When we can see what's in front of us, call it by name, break it down into tiny and manageable steps, clear things off of our task list that don't need to be there and improve things that do, and then ensure our actions are aligned with our values and priorities, that's momentum.

And that, my friend, feels like freedom.

# Chapter 3: Boundary Bloopers

*"You can do anything, but not everything."*
*~David Allen*

## People-Pleasing (source/symptom)

I'm just going to say it now—I'm a recovering people-pleaser. I say recovering because it's still really, really hard for me to say no sometimes.

I worry that people won't like me.

I worry they'll be disappointed.

I worry that they'll think I'm mean. Or uncaring. Or selfish. Or lazy.

I even worry that you'll feel dissatisfied with this book!

And it is so exhausting!

I am getting better—I try to remind myself of that quite often. I've learned that sometimes saying no can be the kindest thing of all. I've learned that when I say no more often, my yes actually means more to people, and I feel less resentment toward people when I actually mean yes, instead of saying yes and thinking, *But my God, you bastards, I am so busy, you better appreciate it!* Oh yeah. That's what goes through my head sometimes. Maybe you can relate.

Many of my clients are just learning how to set and honor boundaries. Boundaries, when done correctly, are nearly always kind. Personal boundaries are about starting to realize what you want to let in and what you want to keep out. When you want to say yes and when you choose to say no. The reality is that learning to recognize and honor our own boundaries reduces resentment, reduces overwhelm and anxiety, and helps us realize what's important to us and in alignment with our own values and priorities. When my clients can learn to honor their own boundaries, their overwhelm paralysis reduces dramatically, because there is simply less on their task list. The things that remain are the things they enjoy.

I remember the first time that I really started to realize that I struggled with respecting my own boundaries—or even knowing what they were and how that was impacting my overwhelm and anxiety level! It was several years ago, and I was working as an administrator for a very busy nursing and rehab facility. It's a twenty-four-hour-a-day job, I had more than one hundred staff members and more than one hundred patients on our campus at any given time, plus all of the family members and loved ones that were coming in to visit. At that time, our company was about to roll out one of the biggest initiatives we'd ever had: a full deployment of an electronic records system, including the migration of all of our current records from 100 percent paper to 100 percent electronic, and a complete retraining for nearly one thousand staff members at twenty-five different locations. I remember getting the call that I needed to head to the home office for a "quick meeting." When I got there, I sat down with my boss and her boss, and I was asked to take the lead as the project manager for the electronic record deployment—while also continuing to do my daily job. It was a huge compliment and a great opportunity to really showcase just how much I could get done in a day. I said yes.

And then I got in my car and cried all the way home.

And then I kept crying all night.

Because I knew it was too much. Oh—did I mention that my kids were four and five years old at the time? And that this project could last anywhere from six months to a year?

But still, I said yes. I knew it might push me over the edge, but I just didn't know what else to do. I didn't want to disappoint my boss. I didn't want to let down our company. I didn't want to look bad or lazy or selfish or like not a team player. I wanted to be liked and admired. I wanted people to think I was perfect—

that I could do it all, and that I could do it all really, really well (okay…I actually wanted them to think I could do it all perfectly). The idea of letting anyone down—anyone at all—made me sick to my stomach. It made my mind race with all of the potential catastrophes that may lurk ahead. I believed that if only I could appease everyone, I would feel less anxious, less stressed, and more secure.

So I did it.

I literally worked nearly sixteen hours a day for six months. I'd get home, put my kids in bed, and get back on my computer to work on the electronic records deployment.

It got done—and, if I do say so myself, it got done well. But I sacrificed quality time with my husband and my children. I sacrificed my health—I didn't have the energy to exercise, and I ate on the fly every day. I sacrificed a little bit of my sanity and my emotional well-being. I was completely out of alignment with my own values, and where I was placing my priority focus. I resented every single minute of it. I resented myself, most of all, for not being brave enough to say "I cannot do this *and do it happily.*"

Part of it was that I wanted to impress my bosses— I wanted to be promoted, I wanted to make more money, I wanted them to think I was totally amazing and the most competent and capable person ever. More of it was that I told myself that I should be able to do it all—I mean…that's what we learn along the way, right? "You can do it all!" And sure…you might be able to, but at what cost? And is it worth it to you?

Why are you saying yes when you want to say no? Are you trying to impress someone or convince them that you are good or good enough (including yourself)? Can you even tune in to what is true for you in that moment, or are you so hard-wired to please others, that yes has become your default?

If you say yes to something, will you be able to keep up with everything else that is on your list? Can you still stay centered around what you truly value? And will you be able to *actually enjoy it*?

At what point do you shift from "it's manageable" to "I'm overwhelmed" and from "calm and confident" to "anxious and stressed"? Because people-pleasing, in reality, is also both a source of anxiety and one of the symptoms. We people-please because we believe it will heal our anxiety, and we feel more anxious because we try to please so many people. Ironic, isn't it?

So if the price isn't worth it, can you say no? *Do you actually know how to say no, and can you risk saying it?*

Can you believe that saying no can actually be the kind thing to do—both for yourself and for the people you care about the most?

And more importantly, how can you tell the difference between a true yes (I actually want to do this!) and a forced yes (I'm going to do this, but I'm going to be pissed off and resentful the whole time)?

My friend and client, Patricia, is a mother, wife, business-owner (and therefore full-time-plus employee), and sits on two different boards of directors. During a recent session, she was talking about her crazy schedule. Prior to this session, we had spent time talking about her values and priorities—one of the things that she had listed at the very top of her values list was spending quality time with her husband and kids on a regular basis, and at the top of her priority list was learning to say no when she just didn't feel up to something.

"This weekend is the first weekend in almost six months that we have nothing planned on our calendar," she told me in passing as we started the session. "But my brother-in-law invited our family over for a BBQ and to spend the night on Saturday. I just don't feel up to it. But we'll probably go."

I stopped her right there. I knew she wanted me to coach her on some organization challenges that were driving her crazy during our session today, but as her coach I knew that how we do anything is how we do everything. I had a hunch that this little bit of small talk was signaling to me what the underlying issue really was. Just like with her brother-in-law, the issues in organizing her calendar and priorities was driving her crazy because she wasn't sure what a real yes was for her! This is where we dove in.

"What do you mean you don't know if you're up for it?" I asked.

"Well… I feel like I should say yes and we should go. We haven't seen them in ages. I don't want to hurt their feelings," she answered.

At this point I wanted to introduce Patricia to the "body compass"—a tool that I learned from the Martha Beck Institute and use regularly with my clients. I think of the body compass as a way to teach my clients to learn to tune into and trust their own intuition. Martha Beck explains the body compass as a game of "warmer/colder" that you might have played as a kid—if you tune into your bodily sensations when you're getting closer to something that you're looking for, or that is right for you (a yes), your body will respond in a positive way (you'll likely feel sensations like relaxing, opening up, feeling lighter)—when you're getting farther away from something that is right for you (a no), you will likely feel physically

47

negative sensations (tightening, heaviness, closing) in different parts of your body.

"Patricia, let's tune into your physical sensations while we talk about this—I'm curious to know how you're actually feeling when we talk about you going to Ryan's house on Saturday night. I just want you to take a few deep breaths and clear your mind first. Now… I want you to think about the upcoming weekend and that you literally have nothing on your calendar or task list to do this weekend. It's completely clear. You have nowhere to go, nowhere to be, you get to sleep in, eat brunch, lay on the couch, watch TV, whatever. As you imagine this weekend with nothing to do, I want you to tell me how you're feeling."

"Oh boy. I feel so relaxed. I'm just completely relieved. I can't even recognize it because I haven't felt this way in so long," she responded. I totally understood—I run into this problem myself pretty regularly!

"Okay, so close your eyes and keep imagining this absolutely free weekend. Describe to me physically how you're feeling—the expression on your face, how your shoulders feel, how your chest feels, how your stomach feels—anything else you notice."

(Patricia is used to this exercise—we've done it before.) "Okay," she answers. "My face feels soft— just relaxed. I actually have a smile on my face. My shoulders are relaxed, and my breathing is slow. I feel kind of a warm feeling in my belly. My hands are unclenched and soft."

"Excellent" I answer. "Now, if you were to picture a horizontal line in front of you with a -10 on the far left end, a zero in the middle being neutral feelings, and a +10 on the far right end being the happiest, best, most wonderful you've ever felt, how are you feeling right now imagining this free weekend?"

"Oh probably a +5! I know it sounds silly to be that happy about...well...literally nothing! But I am!" she answered, laughing.

"Okay, perfect. Now I'm going to have you clear your mind one more time. Go ahead and take a couple of nice slow deep breaths. This time, I want you to imagine the upcoming weekend again, but now it's Saturday, and you're getting ready to load up the family and head to Ryan's house around 3:00 p.m., and you're planning to spend the night there and come home on Sunday morning. Tell me how you're feeling now."

"Ugh. I feel stressed, and actually anxious. I feel awful saying that because I love them, but I feel really tense. Just something on my plate to get ready for, and again, less time at home," she answered.

"Okay—you know the drill—I'd like to know what your physical cues are right now," I told her.

"Well… I'm grimacing. My face is all scrunched up. I'm breathing hard…like it's not slow and relaxed, my breathing is tight and hard. And my shoulders are hunched up by my ears, and I feel heavy in my stomach. I feel anxious and just stressed out. It feels like a -4 on my body compass," she said.

"Okay, so let's talk about this," I answered. "If staying home feels relaxing and stress-free and actually puts a smile on your face, and going to his house makes you feel stressed, anxious, and just general tension, why are you considering saying yes to the invitation?" I asked.

"Well, because I feel bad. We haven't seen them for a long time, and I don't want to hurt his feelings. I don't want them to think that we don't want to hang out with them… I just don't want to hang out with them this weekend. But they won't understand that. I should just say yes—it will cause far less problems and hurt feelings than if I say no."

"Huh…" I responded. "Why are his feelings more important than your feelings? I'm curious."

Silence. "Well…" she finally answered. "They're not *more* important."

"Well, if you're prioritizing his needs above your own, then you are making his feelings more important than yours. You're starting to feel anxious and stressed because you don't want him to be hurt. Can you see that?" I asked.

"Yes… I guess so. But I don't want to be the reason he's upset," she said. I could absolutely relate to this— as a recovering people-pleaser myself, it's painful to feel like someone won't understand your decisions, or to worry and feel anxious that they'll judge you or think you're selfish when you say yes to yourself. Since I have to work through this myself fairly regularly, I felt well-equipped to guide Patricia toward how to make a decision that was a true yes for her over all the other competing voices in her head.

"So if you say yes, and you go over there, but you don't really want to be there in the first place, do you think you'll be the best company?" I asked.

"No—I know that I won't be."

"Will you resent that fact that you're there and not laying on your own couch?" I asked.

"Yes…probably."

"And do you think they won't be able to notice or tell that you're not quite yourself?" I asked.

51

"Well…when you put it that way, they probably will notice."

"So Patricia, is it kinder to go and feel exhausted, stressed, and resentful toward Ryan for inviting you or to say no and actually enjoy being with him the next time you're together?"

"Oh! Ha! Well…it's probably far kinder not to resent him!" she answered, laughing.

Still, Patricia was stuck on the idea that her brother-in-law might have hurt feelings if she said 'no' to the invitation. And I could absolutely relate. She worried he would think she was lazy, selfish, or he would misunderstand her true intentions in saying no. And yet, every time she thought about saying yes, her anxiety and overwhelm crept up on her.

It was at this point that we spent some time discussing Byron Katie's concept of "Your Business, My Business & God's Business" (or the Universe, higher power, etc.'s business).

This is another of my favorite concepts to use with my clients—asking, "Who's business are you in?" and making sure the answer is "Mine!"

"My mom will have hurt feelings if we don't come over for Christmas dinner." You're in your mom's business—that's none of your business. What do *you* want to do for Christmas dinner? *That's your business!*

"My boss will be disappointed if I tell him I don't have the capacity to take on this project." If your boss wants to be disappointed, that's his or her business!

"My hairdresser shouldn't go to Florida on vacation because there might be a tsunami." That's your hairdresser's business. And the tsunami is God's business.

"My friends are going to have hurt feelings if I say no to our monthly bunco night." That's your friends' business.

And in Patricia's case: "Ryan will have hurt feelings if we say no to their invitation." That is none of Patricia's damn business! That's Ryan's business. Patricia's only real job, my only real job, and your only real job is to stay in our own business. But man oh man…is it hard to get out of other people's business. It feels like our moral duty, sometimes, doesn't it?

"Patricia," I finally said. "You cannot control how Ryan feels. That is none of your business. He gets to do and feel whatever the fuck he wants. And you get to do and feel whatever the fuck *you* want! So…what is it that you want?"

"I want to stay at home. Oh boy. I just need to tell him no! He'll get over it. And it literally has nothing to do with him—it has everything to do with me. I just need to rest."

"There! And *now* you are in your own business. You are taking care of your own priorities. Ryan gets to have hurt feelings if he has them, and you get to have your feelings, and from here on out, you can start to practice responding to your own feelings with the same compassion you have always shown for other people. Now, when you say yes to other people, they'll start to realize that it's because you actually want to say yes! How does that feel?"

"It feels...great! Like relief. I don't have to control Ryan's feelings or even try to manipulate them somehow. I get to make my own decision and know that I'm doing it because of me and not because of him. It feels like a lot less pressure on him to entertain me, too!" she answered, laughing.

"So..." I said, getting to the final piece of the task. "What are you going to do now?"

"What do you mean?" she asked.

"Well...are you going to say yes to the invitation, or are you going to say no?" I asked her to get clear about her choice because that's her job. My job is to illuminate options and other perspectives and to give her the tools to find clarity and to find the answer that best serves her. It's none of my business what she chooses—but I am curious!

"Oh...well... I'm going to say no," Patricia answered.

"Okay. When and how?" I asked her, pinning her down now to action. This part helps her to envision actually taking the necessary and hard steps to follow through with the choice she has made. Often, without this step, we all tend to fall back into our more familiar and comfortable patters of, well...anything!

"I hate you," she responded, jokingly. "But okay... I'm going to call him by the end of the day and just let him know that this is our first weekend with nothing on the calendar, and I'm really looking forward to laying low, but that we'd love to set up another time to come out in a few weeks."

"Perfect. I love that in your answer you are owning your decision—when you make a choice that is aligned with your priorities and you stay in your own business, it's a little harder for people to hold it against you. I mean...they can, of course, but most won't—at least not for long. And if they do?"

"It's none of my business," she answered.

"So here's what's great about what we worked on today, Patricia. I know you had wanted to spend a little bit more time talking about how to organize your calendar and commitments so that they aren't driving you to drink, so to speak. Can you see how you can use the body compass tool to take a look at your calendar?" I asked, seeing the opportunity to show Patricia how she could use this tool in many other areas of her life as a means to reduce her anxiety and overwhelm. "What was it, exactly, that was driving you crazy with getting organized?"

"Ha!" Patricia laughed. "Well, actually…it was that there was too much on the calendar, and I feel overwhelmed and stressed out every time I look at it. I want to really get realigned with what I want to be spending my time on."

"Perfect! For your homework between sessions, I'd love for you to use the body compass tool to go back through your calendar and see what you want to keep on there and what you want to say no to. The goal will be to take things off that don't need to be there, in an effort to create more time and space for yourself. Does that sound doable?"

"Absolutely! It's crazy how this stuff all ties back together." Patricia laughed.

"Great. So where would you like to start as far as how you want to tackle this organizing and calendaring challenge and incorporating the body compass and the 3 T's?"

"Hm. Well, I think it makes sense to carve out a few minutes at the beginning of each day and go through my calendar for that day and the next to try to clear up some space by going through each item and finding out if it's something that has to stay or not (note that she's using the 3 T's tool here), and if not, do I *want* it to stay on there by tapping into my body compass."

"That sounds like a good plan. Go ahead and start that tomorrow, and when we regroup next time we can talk about how it went and where I can help you."

I love Patricia's story because it's simple, but the basic tools and principles can be applied just about anywhere in your life (visit www.meaganenglishcoaching.com/uninvitedguest/ to download a body compass tool that I've adapted from the work of Martha Beck and try this for yourself).

First, ask yourself how the decision you're making actually makes you *feel*. Tune in to your own body compass. What are your physical cues telling you? Is your chest tight? Your throat constricted? Your gut heavy? If your physical cues are negative, it's usually the first sign of stress, anxiety, and overwhelm...and if it's stressful, overwhelming, and causes you some kind of anxiousness or pressure, it may not be the right decision. That doesn't mean you can't make it, but it's important to notice how often you are making decisions that are out of alignment for you—because typically that is what those negative feelings are telling you. "This choice may not be good for me." You can still make it, you always have permission to do that—but you might consider giving yourself permission to make the decision that feels stress-free (or at least stress-less).

Second, ask yourself whose business you're in as you're making the decision (this goes back to the "Your Business, My Business, God's Business" concept of Byron Katie's). If you are actually in your own business, you can make the decision that's right for you. When you're in someone else's business, you're almost always making the decision that they would want you to make and ignoring your own needs and desires.

I still struggle with this on the regular. It's a great reminder that learning how to manage our anxiety through reducing our tendency to people-please is an ongoing circle—a loop of learning that we get to practice often before we get the hang of it. As an example, I got a great reminder from my son the other day. I had taken him and a friend down to play at the river near our house—it was pretty busy there with lots of kids and their parents. About an hour in, my son decided he was finished—he simply didn't want to play in the river anymore. His friend was still enjoying himself. My son got out, sat on the shore, and watched his friend play with other kids. "What are you doing? Joe's going to be upset that you're not playing with him!" I admonished.

"He looks fine to me," Landon answered.

"Well, doesn't it bother you that he's playing with other kids, and you're sitting up here all by yourself?" I asked.

"No," Landon answered. "Why would that bother me? I chose to come out here. He chose to stay in there. It's fine, we'll play when he's done."

And all of a sudden I saw it—I was trying to force my son to do something he didn't want to do so no one thought any less of him… I was all up in his business. And his friend's business, too. I was unintentionally passing my own anxiety over the situation on to him! So back to my own business I went.

It's hard to catch, sometimes, and even harder behavior to start to shift, because being a people-pleaser is behavior that we are often externally rewarded for. And yet, so often, it's at an internal cost:

- I don't have time for my family.
- I don't know what I want anymore.
- I am busy all the time and can't take care of my own health.
- I'm overwhelmed. Stressed. Frustrated. Depressed. Anxious. Worried.

I'm still learning how to do this, you guys. So is Patricia. And there are most certainly times that I flounder. Learning how to recognize your boundaries and stop people-pleasing can be a seemingly endless loop of learning, and it can be hard to keep at the forefront of your mind. Sometimes it seems like it's just easier for everyone to say yes...but then what? Then we start saying yes so much that we lose ourselves in the mix again and again—our schedules become sheer back-to-back obligations, with little to no time for the things that actually bring us joy, and we end up, again, frazzled, overwhelmed, and stressed out. This is not easy work—we are not simply kicking a habit. Instead, remember that you're learning to live in a radically free and joyous way. People-pleasing? Yeah, that's a houseguest that might not leave you anytime soon.

But by tapping into your body compass and learning to honor your own boundaries, you can still learn to live alongside those tendencies, and keep them at bay more and more. It can take time to tune back into your body and into your natural intuition—noticing bodily sensations is a practice that most people have become far removed from...and yet, the more you do it, the more you practice, the more your yeses and nos will start to feel like roars rather than gentle whispers. When you start tuning into your heart more than your head, and you begin to practice asking yourself whose business you're in and what your body is telling you, be kind to yourself. Be patient.

Remember that it's practice—not perfection—that matters now.

# Chapter 4: Judge Me, Judge Me Not

*"When you judge another, you don't define them, you define yourself."*
*~Wayne Dyer*

## Fear of Judgment (source)

Perfectionism. Procrastination. People-pleasing. There's a common underlying fear that I hear over and over again when it comes to the topics we talked about in the first three chapters: I just don't want to be judged (or misjudged, as the case may be). Fear of judgement is a source of anxiety—not necessarily a symptom. As such, it is the precursor, at times, to perfectionism, procrastination, and people-pleasing: "I just want to do this exactly right so that people won't judge me or think I screwed up, and also I'm not quite sure where to start or what to do first because I'm not absolutely positive that the result will be perfect, or maybe I just shouldn't do anything, then at least people won't know if I do it wrong, or perhaps instead of doing nothing I should just do what everyone else wants me to do all the time so no one will ever think that I'm lazy or selfish or rude or arrogant or mean or…" Yeah. You probably get the picture.

So here's the real question: Are we being judged? Are *you* being judged?

Remember Zoe and her coworker Steven? Her burning desire to deck him was rooted in the idea that every time he asked her a question, it came from a place of him judging her and her work on the compliance project.

And what about Barrett and the installation of the AC unit? Barrett didn't want to start on the project because he was trying avoid potential judgement from his wife.

And then there's Patricia—amazing, accomplished, smart, wealthy, beautiful Patricia—afraid to say no to anyone or anything for fear that people would judge her for being lazy, selfish, or rude.

Fear of judgement lives in all of us. I delayed a career change that I wanted for nearly five years because I didn't want my friends to judge my decision, my husband to judge me for being selfish or lazy, or my boss to judge me for being a disappointment. The cold hard truth was that I was judging myself for all those things already but was trying to blame everyone else. That may not be your story, but it certainly was mine. When I finally could convince myself that leaving a secure and desirable career to follow my passion and pursue my dreams was not selfish, but would allow me to be generous of self to those I could help; that being an entrepreneur would not allow me to be lazy but would be a different (and far more rewarding) way for me to work my ass off; that creating a new life built of things yet-to-be-learned was not rooted in disappointment but in required bravery—when I finally convinced myself of these things and freed myself of my own judgements, it was miraculous. Not only did I rarely think that other people were judging me, but if they were, I authentically didn't care because I felt aligned with my choice, I wasn't judging myself, and I realized that the people that I needed in my corner would be the ones cheering me on the whole time.

While I can guarantee that your story is not the exact same as mine, it's probably safe to say that there are some broad similarities—and I feel fairly confident in saying so because I uncover a judgement-based fear in every single client I have ever worked with, even when it takes a while to uncover it. One of the fastest ways I have found to identify judgment-based fears is through Equus Coaching™. Equus Coaching™ is an experiential model of coaching, where I invite my clients to interact with a horse in various ways while I observe their behaviors, notice the feedback the horse is offering, identify patterns, and coach them on what we discover. Then the client has the opportunity to try different patterns (or ways of showing up) to see if they can experience new or more desirable results. One of the things I love about working with horses is that it's clear to the client that the horse doesn't have a story about what they should or shouldn't do, and that although the horse is giving feedback, it is completely judgement free. The horse just wants to know it's safe. Like people do. And one way a horse knows that it's safe is that the human in the pen with it has good boundaries: guidelines that identify reasonable, safe, and permissible ways for other people to behave toward them and how they will respond when someone passes those limits. A horse knows it's safe with a human that has good boundaries because it knows what to expect, boundaries are set, and they are honored, without judgment or cruelty. The reality is that there is no way to hide in a round pen with a fifteen-hundred-pound animal.

Recently an extremely accomplished, professional woman named Sandra signed up to work with me. Sandra is married, has two fantastic kids, lives in a desirable neighborhood, takes a couple of well-planned vacations every year, and has an established career with progressive responsibility and a six-figure-income. (I realize that this description of Sandra may make some of you want to punch her in the face from compare-and-despair syndrome, but I assure you, she is a real—and lovely—person). She originally came to work with me as a one-time Equus Coaching™ client—she signed up for a four-hour private session out of "curiosity" and came to the session not quite sure what was on her mind or what she wanted to work on. When she arrived, she told me she was curious, excited, and a little bit nervous. When Sandra arrived to the session, I had some basic background information—I knew what I described above, and I knew that Sandra had worked for the same company for just over ten years and had recently accepted a newly created position in a new division of said company. As Sandra and I were talking, she seemed to be calm, confident, and relatively relaxed.

As we got our session together underway, I invited Sandra to go out into the round pen with our horse partner for the day, a mare named Punkin. From outside the round pen, I asked Sandra how she was feeling, now that she was in the pen with the horse. She said that now that she was in the pen, and I was outside watching her, she felt a little bit more nervous, but still felt generally okay. We talked a bit more, and Sandra shared with me that she had been having a difficult time navigating the new position she was in because she was actually creating it on the fly, and it was so different than her prior position, which she knew so intimately. At this point, I invited her to go ahead and interact with Punkin for a few minutes, to get comfortable in the space she was in, and to try to get Punkin moving a bit in the round pen by trying some different things (knowing that interacting with this horse would be a similar improvisation and would be new and different to her, just like her new job).

Sandra tried a few things, and got Punkin to move a few steps in one direction, and then would stop, think, and try something different, with the result of just another few steps. Every few minutes I noticed her eyes dart over to me, and I could see her taking a breath, and getting more and more tense and nervous as she continued to try to get Punkin to move around the pen with more than just a few steps.

After about four minutes (which I assume felt like a lifetime to her), I asked Sandra to come a bit closer so that I could talk with her.

"Sandra," I started, "I notice as you've been out there working with Punkin that you seem to be getting a little bit of momentum, and then completely changing strategies and starting over. Can you tell me why you're doing that?"

"Oh—I guess I didn't notice that I was doing that, exactly, but now that you say it, it makes sense," Sandra answered. "I was trying to figure out how much movement, how fast, and how long you wanted me to get her moving for, and nothing was working quite as I envisioned it."

"Interesting," I replied. "I also noticed that every minute or so you would glance over at me and seemingly lose whatever connection and momentum you were creating with Punkin. Please tell me if I'm wrong, but you appear to be feeling very stressed right now."

Sandra grimaced slightly. "No—you're right."

"Can you tell me why you were looking over to me?" I asked gently.

"I really don't know," Sandra answered.

"I'm wondering if you were looking over to me because you wanted to know what I was thinking..." I started.

"I..." Sandra started to respond. "I didn't want you to think I was stupid and didn't know what to do." The words came tumbling out of her mouth quickly, as though she was ashamed to even be speaking them.

I smiled at Sandra. "If you did know exactly what to do right off the bat in a situation you've never been in, or had even heard of before, I would be pretty surprised. May I ask you a couple of questions?" I asked.

"Do I have a choice?" Sandra laughed, appearing to feel a bit vulnerable and exposed in this unfamiliar situation.

"Not if you want to get your money's worth here!" I laughed back. "So here's my question: I'm wondering if being in this pen with this horse right now feels anything like your new job, in the sense that perhaps you try a few things and if you don't get immediately impressive results, you quit and change direction?"

"Actually…yes. I know that I do that," she answered.

"And in your new job, when you are worrying about the approval of the people that 'know best,' do you notice that it interrupts the actual momentum you're seeking?" I asked.

At that point Sandra's eyes started to fill with tears. "I just want to make sure that I'm doing the right thing—I don't want my boss to regret giving me this position, and I'm afraid that if I don't figure it out right away, she's going to be disappointed in me or think I'm just not capable of doing it right. I just don't want her to misjudge me or think that I'm not trying—I really am trying! But I'm feeling so stuck and anxious and stressed because I don't know what she's thinking!"

"So while you were out there with Punkin and you were starting to get nervous and anxious, what were you thinking?" I asked.

"That you must think I'm an idiot," Sandra answered shyly.

"I assure you, I don't—but we can come back to that in a minute if you'd like. Is that the same thing you're fearing that your boss must be thinking about you? That she thinks you're an idiot?"

"No. I'm thinking that she's going to regret having me in this position."

"Why?" I asked curiously.

"Because I can't figure this out."

"And you think you should be able to figure it out right now?" I asked.

"Well yes! I should be able to figure this out right now—it's my job!" she responded—looking tearful, anxious, and stressed.

At that point, Sandra's calm, cool façade was being disrupted by feelings of "not good enough" and fears of being judged—pardon me for saying so, but now I had her right where I wanted her (and I mean this in the most loving, supportive, and encouraging way possible!). It felt like the perfect time to introduce her to a variation of the "Thought Work" of Byron Katie. In a nutshell, here's the process I used:

1) Find the painful thought—the one that's causing the stress/anxiety/discomfort.

71

2) Ask yourself if that thought is actually true— as in, do you know, without a shadow of a doubt, that it is 100 percent unequivocally true.

3) Tap into that wise wisdom of the "body compass" and consider how you feel when you believe that thought—and is it helping you in any way?

4) Consider some alternate perspectives (Katie calls this step 'Turnarounds').

5) Establish some evidence for these other perspectives.

6) Find a belief or perspective to hold on to that feels true and doesn't stress you out nearly as much!

Back to Sandra:

"Okay—are you *absolutely sure* that your boss is judging you for not having your job all figured out *right now*?" I asked.

"Well…I mean, I believe it. Is that what you mean?" Sandra asked me.

"Yeah, I can see that you believe that it's true—but I'm asking you if you *know for sure*, without a doubt, that your boss is judging you and thinking that you should *absolutely* have this *whole job* all figured out *right now*. I'm not asking you if you *think* it's true. I'm asking you if you know that for a fact."

"Oh. Well...no. It's not as though she's said that to me or has told me that it had to be all figured out by a certain date."

"Did anyone say to you that you need to have this 100 percent figured out at all?"

"Uh...no," Sandra responded.

"Okay—so when you're believing that you have to have it all figured out right now, and if you don't, your boss must be judging you, how do you feel?" I asked.

I noticed Sandra becoming teary again. "Just...awful. I feel inadequate and lazy and ashamed...and like I should try harder, but I don't know why or how. I feel really stressed and anxious. My stomach hurts and my neck hurts. Ugh. It's a terrible feeling, like I'm just under all this pressure and judgment."

"And when you're feeling this way, do you feel like you're performing at your best?"

"Oh no! Not at all—I feel totally distracted and like I can't pick a direction or stick with a decision because I'm so scared if it's the right decision."

I smiled. "Kind of like interacting with Punkin out there?"

"Yes! Just like that!" Sandra looked astonished.

73

"So if everything was the same—you were still in this brand-new position in this brand-new division with a new-to-you boss, but you just knew that you shouldn't actually have it all figured out right now and that your boss isn't looking at you and judging you to be lazy or inadequate because you don't have it all figured out right now, how do you think you might feel or behave differently?" I asked Sandra.

"Well…" she paused and looked around. "I think that if I knew my boss wasn't watching me and judging any misstep, I might be more willing to try some different things, see them through, and see if they work. I might actually make more progress because I'm not afraid to see the end result." As she was talking I noticed she was growing more animated and her confidence appeared to be returning. "Actually, I think it might be fun to figure it out, if I didn't think I should already have it figured out, that is."

"Do you think you would feel less anxious? Less stressed? Less pressure? Less fear of judgment and therefore more enthusiasm for what you're doing?"

"Absolutely!" she responded enthusiastically. "I would be able to take one thing at a time, and I wouldn't necessarily equate making a mistake to being a total failure."

"Wow—that sounds like a relief." I responded.

"Yeah…actually just talking about it that way feels like a relief."

"Could it be, Sandra, that the opposite is true? That your boss isn't judging you for not having it all figured out right now?"

"Hm. Maybe." Sandra responded, unconvinced. I don't blame her—I use this process with myself all the time, and I am often unconvinced (at first).

"Challenge time!" I announced. "I'd like you to give me three real examples of how your boss isn't judging you for not having it all figured out right now."

"What?! What do you mean?" Sandra laughed.

"I'll help you with one to start. Try this: 'My boss isn't judging me for not having it all figured out right now when she's too busy worrying about her own stuff.'"

"Oh! Well, that is true! She probably is too busy to be thinking about me!" she laughed.

"Okay—your turn." I instructed. "You can just state the sentence and add 'if' or 'when' at the end before you establish the evidence. Give it a try. I want at least two more examples of how it could be true that your boss isn't actually judging you for not having it all figured out right now."

"Hm. Okay…so my boss isn't judging me for not having it all figured out right now when it's a brand-new position, and I've only been in it for three months. And…I shouldn't have it all figured out right now when I want to take my time and do it right."

"Awesome. Anything else?"

"Well…yeah… My boss isn't judging me for not having it all figured out right now if I have enough figured out for now to move forward!" Sandra answered, looking pleased.

"I love that! So let me ask you—when you think about it in those terms, do you think it's equally as true, or possibly even truer, that your boss isn't judging you and that you actually shouldn't have it all figured out right now?"

"Yes! I do think it's truer! How funny… It seems so obvious that there is no way I should have it all figured out right now when we talk about it this way, and that it's highly unlikely that my boss is spending all of her time thinking about me." Sandra answered.

"And when you believe that, the idea that you actually shouldn't have it all figured out right now and that your boss isn't judging you for it—how do you feel?" I asked.

"I feel so much better! I feel calm and confident—way less sick to my stomach. I feel relaxed. It feels so good to take that pressure off myself and just the worry over what my boss must be imagining."

"So is there any action you'd like to take from here relative to how you're feeling in this new role, and how you can keep the pressure in check?" I asked Sandra, as we got ready to move into the next portion of our session.

"You know, actually I think I'd like to try to schedule a meeting with my boss to get her perspective on how I'm doing and outline some actual goals, so that I'm not making stuff up along the way." Sandra responded.

Sandra's story is a great example of how our minds create problems that may not even exist—and she's definitely not alone.

When we can start to recognize the power that our beliefs have on us and start to uncover where there is truth and where there is a murky tendency to believe something that's ultimately painful, unproven, and generally limiting to our happiness, we can start to see those thoughts for what they are and undo those damn made-up mind tricks.

"My boss will regret hiring me."

"My friends will never invite me out again."

"My husband will think I'm selfish."

"My client will think I'm lazy."

"My kids will think I'm a terrible mother."

"My staff will think I'm mean."

First of all, remember that what s/he/they think of you is absolutely none of your business. Then do me a favor: ask yourself if that thing you're believing is actually true. Is it helping you, or is it hurting you? Look at it from another perspective (the opposite is the easiest…but there are others that I work with my clients on as well). Establish some evidence to support this new perspective. See if it feels better. If it does, keep it and wave good-bye to the unhelpful thought your mind created for you.

And if you have a kaleidoscope of butterflies burning anxious knots into your belly and you'd like to explore whether I can help you to let those suckers fly, email me at meagan@meaganenglishcoaching.com to sign up for a complimentary thirty-minute strategy session with me. I'd love to see if I can support you to walk with your anxiety and learn how to embrace your calm, cool, confident self.

# Chapter 5: I Can See Clearly Now...

*"It's not hard to make decisions once you know what your values are."*
*~ Roy E. Disney*

## Clarity and Decision-Making
(source/symptom)


If you've ever felt stuck, you should know that you're not alone. It doesn't matter if you feel stuck in your career, stuck in your marriage, stuck in your life, or just stuck in a rut—when you've been doing the same thing in the same way for a long time, it's hard to see a way out.

Even more challenging can be those times when you know you want a way out, but you know that what you have is pretty good—you might think of it as the "grass isn't always greener" phenomenon. Sometimes this "stuckness" itself can cause us to feel anxious, stressed, and overwhelmed because we can't quite figure out how to get out of it. Being stuck and feeling without direction is a source of anxiety that I can relate to oh-so well.

By the time I had been in my former career for more than ten years, I was in a bit of a "grass isn't always greener" conundrum: I worked for an awesome company in a great job that many people would love, making an enviable income, and I was really good at it. I didn't hate it at all. I just didn't love it. The question that ran through my mind for the next several years was, "Is this it? Is this all there is? You go to a job that you're good at and is okay and then you die?" And every time, I answered myself in one of the same two ways: either "sounds really lame" or "you idiot, what if you try something else and it's *so* much worse?" In both scenarios, I had convinced myself that I could just never really know.

I felt stuck—and in turn silly, anxious, and confused—because I had convinced myself that nothing was really that bad…something was just wrong with me.

You see, I didn't wake up every morning and dread going to the office—I just wasn't excited.

I worked with people that were kind, respectful, and smart—I just didn't always feel like I unequivocally belonged.

I knew I was doing meaningful work—but I was not passionate about it.

And the problem? I actually didn't know (or didn't think I knew), what I was passionate about. So I started guessing—and anxiously guessing about your passions simply isn't a very effective or stress-free strategy. The more I agonized over what to do, the more anxious I got and the less clearly I could think.

It wasn't until I started working with my own coach that I realized two things:

1) I could probably find a way to discover and ignite my passions in ways outside of work that would make me happier and more satisfied in my work life.
2) I didn't want to do #1.

That story line might well be different for you—but I have found that one thing rings true for all my clients (and my family and friends too, for that matter). Life is too short to live out of alignment with your values and out of integrity with who you are and what makes you happiest. When you do live in that way, your body (and your mind—that anxious and protective mind) will let you know in any number of ways, including but not limited to, you guessed it, anxiety. However yours manifests—sleeplessness, a knot in your stomach, an inclination to turn down invitations or accept every invite that comes your way—usually stems from a place of not knowing.

Whether we're talking about your career or business, your hobbies or your relationships, one thing has become clear to me. First you must know what your values are. Then you can mentally adjust your priorities. Finally, you can act. Trying to do these things out of sequence typically results in more stress, more anxiousness, and more pressure—but doing them in sequence? Sweet relief. In this way, you can learn to live alongside your anxiety—you may not be kicking it out of the house, so to speak, but you can recognize what's allowing it to take over, and in turn, you can start to calm it—and yourself.

My client Michelle is a great example of someone who struggles with this very phenomenon: directionless-ness. Michelle worked her way up from a midlevel management position to an executive level position in a national manufacturing firm. She moved across the country, left a marriage, and started her own private marketing business…until she moved back across the country, accepted a VP-level position in a completely different industry than she'd ever worked in before, got remarried, and started a family. Then she restarted her own business again (on the side), and started participating in an MLM (multilevel marketing) company on the side of that. Why? Let's find out…

When Michelle and I first started working together, she was struggling to make a decision about the volume of work she was doing and juggling that with her marriage and raising her daughter. She wasn't sure what to keep, what to let go of, what to start, or what to stop. Although she knew what she didn't like, she couldn't tell me what she did like. She enjoyed the money that came from these various endeavors, but she didn't need the money. She liked that everyone admired her for doing so much, but she wasn't really sure she admired herself. I had a hunch that the reason that Michelle was struggling to make decisions about how much (and where) to work was because she wasn't in tune with what she actually wanted. She had simply never spent much time thinking about the end goal of what she was trying to accomplish.

"Tell me about how you're spending your time right now, Michelle," I invited on our very first call.

"I spend a lot of time working. A lot. Actually, almost all of my time is spent working. And I can get it all done—I can get more done in a day than most people can in three days. I'm just starting to get a little bit tired and overwhelmed, and I'm starting to wonder if I should cut back on something so that I can be more available to Anna as she gets older."

"I'm curious why you are doing all of these things right now. The day job, the private practice, and the MLM sales—what's driving that?"

"Well…I love cooking, which is why I started doing the MLM sales. I love helping people with that. Also, I make about a thousand dollars a month by doing that, so it helps pay for my car. As far as my own practice, I want to be able to get my own practice up and running alongside my job so that I can eventually just do that and have my own hours and the freedom to work when and where I want to. And I just can't afford to quit my day job now. We have a lifestyle that requires that income, and we don't want to give that up."

As Michelle was talking, she sounded unconvinced in some way, to me, and there was an increased speed at which she talked that told me she was starting to get a bit anxious the more she talked about all of these competing priorities. At this point I had a pretty clear sense that Michelle's motivation in doing these three jobs was driven by a desire for continued financial success, but in order to help her get clarity and decide if she wanted to keep doing things the same way, or if she wanted to let go of something, I decided to walk her through the body compass exercise (placing herself into specific scenarios and having her tell me how those scenarios made her feel on a scale of -10 to +10). If you remember, our body compass can help us to identify what options we have and which ones cause more and less stress and anxiety response in our physical cues.

Once we ran several scenarios through the body compass awareness exercise, Michelle had discovered that she enjoyed doing MLM, but to pursue it full-time and give up something else would be a negative experience for her because of the financial pressure, while keeping a focus on maintaining MLM work for a couple of hours a day was actually neutral.

The final scenario that I asked Michelle to imagine herself in was reducing some of her MLM time, allowing 1–2 hours per day for something else, but keeping it as a hobby. "Okay—now let's shift for a minute—I want you to imagine that you're sleeping in until 6 a.m., you are only doing the things on MLM that you like to do but you're not actually trying to grow that business, and there's no pressure to get up any earlier or devote more time than you have—you choose what you want, and some days that might be nothing. But you still go to your day job. Where is that on your body compass?" I ask.

"Okay…that's really odd…it's like a +3. But I thought I loved doing MLM!" she said, surprised.

"Yes," I laughed. "And you can still do it! But it seems as though taking the pressure off it feels better to you."

For Michelle, the body compass helped her see which of her activities was actually bringing her joy versus causing more stress—and then we could start to create a dialogue around the real reasons that she was holding on to MLM so tightly (which turned out to be fear of failure and fear of judgment—both sources of anxiety, alongside the feeling of being stuck and directionless).

After spending the next several sessions working through some of the related revelations Michelle had had about the fears she was experiencing, we circled back around so that I could help her get a clearer vision of what was at the root, what was driving her, and ultimately to what she wanted from her future. While Michelle could discern her "warmer" and "colder," she was having a hard time articulating (to me and to herself) what she wanted to gain from all of this work in the future.

To gain more clarity and help Michelle tap into her desires and what she envisioned for her future, I introduced a visualization exercise called the "Ideal Day" (which I originally learned through my training at the Martha Beck Institute). Meditation and visualization are commonly used by top executives and professional athletes to aid in enhancing performance, and they can also help us become more aware of our subconscious processing. Because our conscious mind only processes about forty bits of information per second and our subconscious mind processes closer to four million bits of information per second, it is valuable to try to access some of that vast information that we humans don't pay attention to much of the time. The "Ideal Day" exercise helps clients tap into the dreams that they might avoid acknowledging out loud, or might not even be aware of. With it, I help clients uncover how they would love to spend their time if they were not afraid to take a leap, or alternately to find out what the optimal use of their time would be and find a way to incorporate more of that into their current world.

Because I knew Michelle to be more comfortable with "left-brained" (logical, analytical, and objective) inquiry, I hoped that the Ideal Day exercise could really help her let loose and explore what she might like to find in her own future. By helping Michelle to tap into the unspoken or unrecognized dreams of her subconscious, we could learn more about what drives her, what truly motivates her, and what brings her joy. Once we had this information, we could start to integrate some of those optimal elements into her life right now.

"Michelle," I suggested at the next session. "I'd like to do an exercise with you—it's a guided visualization where I help you to envision what an optimal work day might hold for you at some point in the future. What do you think?" I asked.

"I've never done anything like that before, so sure—it might be interesting!" she laughed.

"Awesome. I'd like you to get really comfortable wherever you are—we're going to tap into your subconscious a little bit—there's a lot of information that we humans keep in there that we're not always great about tapping into. There's a lot of scientific evidence about meditation and visualization and how it can help us to perform better," I shared with her, knowing that her analytical mind may need a little reassurance about why we were doing this. "Picture your brain as a little snow globe, and all of those little flakes are bits of information in our subconscious that we're going to try to catch right now, using visualization."

"Sounds weird, but it makes sense—let's go for it!" Michelle laughed.

For the next twenty minutes, I helped guide Michelle through her optimal work day by asking her questions and seeing where she imagined herself spending time and what she imagined herself doing, if there were no strings attached, no right or wrong, no judgement. Michelle's job was simply to keep her eyes closed, imagine, and respond to the questions that I was asking without thinking about the answer.

When we were finally done with the exercise, I asked Michelle to open her eyes, and I read my notes back to her. In the visualization, she had imagined herself about five years into the future, still working for the same company but in a slightly different role. She wasn't spending any time in her private practice. She had also not expanded her MLM practice but had maintained it through just a few hours a week. I noted she had said that her husband had started his own company. They also had two children in this optimal future and traveled a bit less, but still at least twice a year.

After sharing my notes with Michelle, I asked her what stood out to her, and what—if anything— surprised her about what she had envisioned.

"The thing that is standing out to me is that MLM can just stay a hobby—the reason I was trying to grow it was for everyone else and not me, but ultimately what I'd obviously prefer to do is just make enough money and get enough satisfaction from my day job so that I don't have to have pressure on the other things. I'm not ready quite yet to give up my private practice... I still want to see where that goes, but I'm not going to let it consume my life. That will all save me so much time and relieve so much pressure." Contemplating not only her awareness from the Ideal Day exercise, but also the work of priorities, body compass, and judgement awareness from the previous several sessions, Michelle erupted with "Oh my gosh! That also means I don't have to go to the MLM conference this summer! I was *dreading* it, but I thought I had to be there if I wanted to grow my business! What a relief—just that one thing coming off my plate feels so much better!" she answered, sounding one thousand pounds lighter. "It's interesting to me that I've never really sat down and talked through my goals, priorities, and hopes for the future with anyone before. Honestly, I think I would have been embarrassed to say that my priority was financial for now, had you not flat-out asked me. And I never would have imagined reducing my MLM focus because I just didn't want people to think I had failed. I'm excited to get a little more time with Anna now—and maybe even a little sleep. I feel really good about the shifts I'm about to make and why I'm going to make them. I feel so much less anxious now that I actually have a direction to go and understand why I'm going that way!"

"There is no wrong value or priority," I reminded Michelle. "The only problem comes in when we don't know or acknowledge them honestly, because then we don't have direction in how we are spending our time. Now that you've been able to create a little more awareness using your body compass, visualizing a positive future through the Ideal Day, and simple acknowledgement about your priorities and values, you can create a direction that feels good to you, and that's all we were trying to do."

Wouldn't you know it, just three months after we worked through this, Michelle was offered an opportunity with her employer to take on oversight of the wellness division for her company. This new position not only bolstered her income impressively, but it allowed Michelle to drop the MLM obligation to hobby status—which is exactly what she'd envisioned in her "Ideal Day" exercise! She was able to focus on helping people with their health and wellness—a passion of hers—and meet her financial objectives (her priority) through her day job! By identify her values, stating her passions, and clearly imagining the future she was hoping for, Michelle not only found more freedom of time, but is happier than she's ever been, not only in her career, but in her life overall. The overwhelm and stress that she was feeling from her former schedule, and the anxiety that came from not knowing why she was doing what she was doing or where she was going to go with it, are all taking up much less space in her mind and on heart, because she has learned how to live more fully and freely. And that, my friends, is a win for us both.

# Chapter 6: Failure vs. Feedback

*"It is she who has enough confidence to define success and failure for herself who succeeds."*
*~Sophia Amoruso*

## Fear of Failure (source)

Michael Jordan.

Oprah Winfrey.

Steve Jobs.

Steven Spielberg.

Walt Disney.

Jack Canfield.

The Beatles.

Do you know what all of these people have in common? Besides the fact, of course, that they are all wildly famous, rich, and successful.

Take a guess.

Give up? I'll tell you: they all failed. They failed on a pretty impressive scale, too, most multiple times, to get to the point of "wildly famous, rich, and successful." The difference between these people and me (and maybe you too) is how they view failure. For most of my life, my failures (and fear of failure) caused a huge spike in my level of anxiety—high-functioning and unrelenting anxiety. Them? They used it as feedback and opportunity—they viewed failure differently, and therefore they used it differently. What causes anxiety for me, they used as a platform for opportunity, learning, expansion, and growth.

What exactly do I mean?

Michael Jordan was cut from his high school varsity basketball team, and over the course of his career he missed more than nine thousand shots. Today? He's widely considered one of the best basketball players of our time. "I've failed over and over and over again in my life…and that is why I succeed."[2]

Oprah Winfrey was once fired for being "not right for television" and too emotional. That didn't stop her—she went on to create and host one of the highest-ranking shows (*The Oprah Winfrey Show*) in American history and later developed *O* Magazine and the OWN Network. Not to mention, she's an incredible philanthropist and one of the richest and

---

[2] Michael Jordan, "Failure" commercial, https://www.youtube.com/watch?v=JA7G7AV-LT8.

most influential women in the world. Her take on failure? "There's no such thing as failure, really, because failure is just that thing trying to move you in another direction—so you get as much from your losses as you do from your victories. The losses are there to wake you up!"[3]

Steve Jobs—you know the guy—the famous former CEO of Apple and all things "i"? Before becoming a household name, he had been restricted in duties at Apple (for allegedly wanting to take Apple in the wrong direction), ultimately stepped down from his duties as Chief Visionary, and then was asked to return in an even more incredible role and turn of fortune. Jobs once said: "I didn't see it then, but it turned out that getting fired from Apple was the best thing that could have ever happened to me. The heaviness of being successful was replaced by the lightness of being a beginner again, less sure about everything. It freed me to enter into one of the most creative periods of my life."[4]

Before becoming a critically acclaimed, influential, and well-known writer, producer, and director, Steven

---

[3] Oprah Winfrey on Career, Life, and Leadership at Stanford School of Business https://www.youtube.com/watch?v=JA7G7AV-LT8.

[4] Stanford News Steve Jobs Commencement Speech, 2005, http://news.stanford.edu/2005/06/14/jobs-061505/.

Spielberg was rejected in his application to attend film school. Twice.

The "happiest place on Earth" (and all other things Disney) was created by Walt Disney, but only after he was fired at age twenty-two from a newspaper for not being creative enough and subsequently suffered bankruptcy in one of his earliest ventures.

If you've never heard of the Chicken Soup for the Soul books, I'm sorry—they're fantastic. Also, you might want to climb out from under that rock that you've apparently been living under. In any case, Jack Canfield, that persistent and amazing bastard, was rejected 144 times before he found a publisher for his first Chicken Soup for the Soul book! *144 times!* The publisher that finally did pick it up, however, must be thrilled, because Jack's first book, when finally published, sold more than eight million copies in America, ten million copies around the world, and his brand is now a billion-dollar brand. (You guys…seriously…help me do that, m'kay?)

"Yellow Submarine," "I Want to Hold Your Hand," "Twist and Shout": had the Beatles given up or been afraid to try again after being rejected by record labels, and told, "We don't like your sound" and "Guitar music is on its way out," some of the world's most beautiful music may never have found its way into our homes, hearts, and heads (where sometimes we can't get it out… I bet you're humming "We All Live In A Yellow Submarine" right now, aren't you?).

I'm going to stop there, but I most certainly could go on—there are more incredible stories of people just like those I've mentioned here that failed—famously—and went on to do exactly what they set out for…or something different. The point is that they didn't let setbacks stop them from going after their dreams.

So why do so many of us let that fear—the fear of failure—hold us back? The real truth is that many of us don't even know that's what it is. We just tell ourselves that what we have is good enough—and sometimes it is. Ironically, I often tell people that I'm working with that "good enough" can be both "good" and "enough"… It can also, however, be the crutch you're relying on to stay right where you are. Sometimes it takes an outside perspective to see the difference.

Part of the problem tends to be how we view success, which is why one of my favorite exercises is to have clients redefine success for themselves. I help them expand their definition to include both quantitative and qualitative elements. Had you asked me how I would know when I was successful a few years back, as an example, I would have ticked off several items for you (all of which caused varying degrees of anxiousness, should I not meet these predefined goals):

- Once I achieve a six-figure income, I'll be successful.
- At the point that I am promoted until I can't be promoted anymore, I'll feel successful.
- When I can stop living within a budget, I'll consider myself successful.

And so I kept trudging along—driven by money, yes. But also by ego and by a quantitative definition of success that I'd never really stopped to think twice about.

When I did stop to think about it, that was when it all changed. Please don't misunderstand—I am an unashamed money-lover. I love to have cash, I like to put dollars into my retirement fund, I detest thinking about budgets, and I feel thrilled when I can go on vacation and feel completely at ease. But now, I realize there are other things that are equally, and in some cases, more important to me—and I've learned that those items are a fundamental part of my now-definition of success, which is as follows:

- Financial freedom: Being able to afford not only what is required, but being able to indulge when I choose to, without guilt or fear.

- Being an equitable contributor to my household: Part of that is financial (see financial freedom above), but to me this also means having the time and space to participate in the daily workload (dishes, sweeping, laundry, meal preparation), and actively raising our children.
- Freedom of schedule: Being able to choose *not to work* when my kids are at home and awake.
- Self-health and physical well-being: Going to bed at a decent hour, getting a good night's sleep, reducing my alcohol intake, and setting aside time for physical movement each day.

Notice that my definition of success does not exclude a financial element, or the "ego" element—both of those items are important to me and therefore stay on my list (yes—my regular pedicure is non-negotiable—the housekeeper, however, I was willing to get rid of...temporarily). What it does not include are the other things that I had simply been ignoring as I pursued the American Dream: my own dreams.

I have just a touch of a distractibility condition—which means I get bored by doing the same thing over and over. So my former job, while not in any way boring in the traditional sense, was simply not that interesting to me anymore after 10+ years in the making. So what did that tell me? That it was time to make a change. And why didn't I? Failure. Or fear of failure, rather. I was so paralyzed, overwhelmed, and anxious by the idea that I would leave what was good enough, good, and enough, and go sink into a snake pit of my own making, that I just stayed put.

The result? Exactly the opposite of what I now define as successful—go figure! I was financially free, sure. But I did not contribute equitably to my household (except for financially), I worked all the time (my phone was literally never more than three feet from my hand), I did not have the freedom to choose my schedule for the most part, and I was in no way focusing on self-health or my physical well-being (I never exercised, I went to bed late, and then woke up at all hours of the night, I drank too much, I ate too much, I was rarely or never outside…you get the gist).

But I took comfort in the fact that I was *very successful. S*o why would I make a change? I wouldn't, and I didn't. For a good long while.

If you're curious, I'd like you to do this "Success Definition" exercise right now: Create your own definition of success by writing down 3–5 bullet points. At least half of them should be qualitative and not quantitative. Now let's see where you're measuring up, and where you've got some work to do, because if you're achieving financially but you're waking up anxious in the night or feeling stuck, that probably means that there is some element of success that is yet unfulfilled for you. My guess is that, if there are measures of success that you're not pursuing, it's possible that there is a fear of failure issue that might be holding you back and causing you to feel anxious, overwhelmed, and paralyzed, to some extent.

So let's take a look—once you've created your own definition of success, I'd like you to comb through it and see where you'd like to do better. If there's an area, or a bullet point, where you're falling shy of what's important to you, ask yourself why. What is it that's stopping you? If it's a fear of failing, ask yourself why that is scaring you—what exactly are you making failing at something mean—about you, about your life, about your dreams, or about your vision?

Specifically, I want you to ask yourself one thing: *What would you do if you knew you could not fail?* Let yourself imagine and admit the unthinkable. What would you do?

I'd like you to meet my client, Fisher. Fisher is a very cool cucumber, in his mid-thirties, and married with two young children. He works in technology, lives in a hip, urban neighborhood, and is a contributing member of the middle-class, making just upward of $60,000 annually. When Fisher and I first met, he had been working in the same job at the same company for just under ten years. As part of my intake process with clients, I ask them to complete an application so that I can gain an understanding of what it is they'd like some support with, followed by a complimentary consultation to clarify the potential client's goals and discover whether we're a good fit.

As I was reviewing Fisher's application for coaching, two things became immediately clear to me:

1) Fisher believed that he was hiring me, point-blank, to help him strategize, prioritize, and take-action. Those things would definitely be true.

2) There was an underlying and somewhat unacknowledged theme to Fisher's application: unpursued dreams of spending his time creatively and musically.

As Fisher and I started our consultation call, I asked him a few clarifying questions about what he was having trouble with and where he envisioned me being able to best support him.

"Well, I always have great ideas—amazing ideas! At home, at work… I love to come up with ideas. But for some reason, I have a lot of trouble starting things—and when I do start them, the reality is that they almost never get finished," Fisher told me.

"Is this primarily at home, at work, elsewhere, or…everywhere in your life?"

"It's everywhere. I'm driving my wife crazy—there are unfinished projects literally all over the house, and my boss brings it up to me every year in my evaluation. I know I'm well-liked, I'm smart, and I know technology, but when it comes to new things I just can't get moving."

I immediately identified a few things that I believed could be true for Fisher. One was that it sounded like he was having "overwhelm paralysis"—the ability to start with the end in mind, as Stephen Covey tells us, but then the inability to break the process down into manageable steps. Fisher was having grandiose ideas, and that's exactly where they were staying. Stacked on top of the issue of potential "Overwhelm Paralysis", the other thing I suspected might be true for Fisher was that his ideas meant so much to him and were so important that he was afraid if he didn't execute them perfectly it would be an immeasurable disappointment—both to him and to the other people around him—the perfectionist tendencies and desire not to be judged as inadequate that we talked about earlier. And finally, I suspected that Fisher had a major aversion to failure and that he probably believed that by not pursuing anything, he'd avoid failing altogether. These three tendencies combined contributed to Fisher experiencing constant stress and anxiety about what he should be doing and how to do it successfully (as in—how to avoid failure). As a coach, I know that most of my clients need to work their way through these various tendencies at their own pace and that it's my responsibility to point out observations that I think will best serve my client in the moment.

I decided to talk with Fisher a little bit about my theory of "overwhelm paralysis" to start with and go from there.

"Fisher, based on everything you've told me and what I reviewed in your application, I believe I have some ideas and tools that would really benefit you, and I'd love to work with you. Not only do I think that we'll be able to work on some of the things that you've identified are challenges for you, I also suspect we'll be able to improve your life in ways you may not even have thought of yet! One of the first things that comes to mind as I'm listening to you is this idea that you have so many things on your list that you have a hard time taking action or prioritizing—I like to refer to this as 'overwhelm paralysis,' and it's something many of my clients struggle with. I suggest we start there and see where our sessions take us, though I'm noticing some other themes that I'd like to circle back to. I like to work in a very organic way, since everyone is different—your job will be to show up ready to talk about whatever is weighing on your mind, stressing you out, or pissing you off, and then to be willing to practice 'homework' that we identify together between sessions. My job is to hold space, listen, ask questions that help you to think more deeply about things, make observations, offer perspectives and ideas, and serve as an accountability partner and motivator. My other job is to make sure that if I notice thought and behavior patterns showing up for you that I believe it might be beneficial to become aware of and consider shifting, I point those out to you. You may not always like me during sessions, but I'm okay with that—my job is to help you get the most of our time together. How does that sound to you?"

"Amazing. Really, I feel excited and relieved just talking through this. I can't wait to get started," Fisher replied.

Over the course of the next several months, Fisher and I worked through several of the areas that I had identified based on his application and consultation. While he was making progress, I noticed that it still felt like he was holding something back. He showed up to every session with something to work on, prepared to reflect on how his homework went over the prior time period, and he was reflective, curious, and honest, so I couldn't quite pinpoint why I felt like we could go a bit deeper than we were going.

During our fifth session, Fisher started sharing with me that he had been asked to create a solution to a technology problem and present it at a staff meeting.

He'd been given carte blanche to be as creative as he wanted to be and ultimate freedom of how to get where he wanted to go, so long as he solved the technology problem. He was paralyzed.

"I don't have enough information to execute this correctly, I want to present a perfect product, and if I don't, my boss will be disappointed. I'm so frustrated I can't even start working on it," Fisher vented.

"Hm," I let out. "I'm a little perplexed, and I'll tell you why. One of the things that came across over and over to me in your application was this deep desire to be creative and to have opportunities to tap into that creativity. Now you've been given an opportunity to do just that—to be as creative as you want with a solution and to present it to the team however you want. So why are you frustrated?"

"Because I don't know if it's going to be right!" Fisher nearly exploded.

"Why does it have to be right?" I asked.

"Because," Fisher stubbornly answered, starting to feel his frustration simmering.

"Because why? Take your time here. I'm not in a rush. I'm just curious why it's so important that you do it exactly right."

At this point I could sense something changing on the other end of the phone line, and when Fisher started speaking again, I could hear his voice shaking with emotion. "I just don't want people to judge me for doing it wrong," he let out, and then I could hear the deep breaths that signal emotion from the other end of the line.

"What do you think it means if someone judges you for doing it wrong?" I asked.

"That I'm a failure," Fisher practically choked out.

"And why is it so terrible to fail?" I asked, gently.

This time the silence was so long, I almost had to ask if he was still there. Until...

"Honestly," Fisher said, sounding much calmer. "I don't know? I just feel sick when I think about being seen as a failure. I feel this overwhelming anxiety."

"Okay—this is so great that we've uncovered this. I'd like to work on this a lot more going forward, but for now I really would like you to start trying to think of failure a little bit differently. What if what you are thinking of as failure is simply feedback that you should do or try something a slightly different way? How would that feel for you?" I asked.

"Well...it doesn't sound nearly as catastrophic," Fisher answered, starting to laugh a little bit.

"So when you think about creating and proposing this solution and then envisioning it being this giant failure, I think we know the result that's having—it's keeping you from starting and totally blocking your creativity, but tell me where I'm wrong."

"No…that's right—I can't even get started thinking about it because all I can think of is to avoid failure at all costs!"

"Fisher, when you think about creating and proposing this solution, and one of the potential outcomes is that your boss says to you, 'That's not what I was looking for,' but you see that as feedback and an opportunity to clarify and try something different, how do you think you might behave differently right now?" I asked.

"Actually…it makes me want to just try something so that I can see what comes out of it, and if I get feedback that it's not quite right, then at least I know! It's a lot less stressful," Fisher said.

"Great—so let's just start with this one project and this one situation and see if in this specific scenario we can frame up the idea of failure just a little bit differently and see how it goes. We can get broader from here as we go along," I said, encouraging Fisher to keep it small, and knowing that it was too soon to ask him to start self-identifying where he could reframe this idea of failure on his own just yet. One of the things most of my clients, and I, tend to do is want to overhaul everything at once. The reality is that we've built an entire lifetime of patterns, habits, and ways of being and doing…and to start to un-learn these things takes time and guidance. It is a continuous unfolding and repeating of learning new ways to think, behave, and live. I like to challenge my clients with tasks, projects, and shifts, but I also want them to experience the small successes, build on them, and understand that these small steps are what lead to big change. As we learn to live alongside our anxiety and the pressures we navigate, the ultimate goal is to feel and live more freely and peacefully, moment by moment and day by day.

Over the course of the next nine months that Fisher and I continued to work together, we revisited this fear of failure issue regularly, we noticed the anxiety and paralysis that it produced within him, and we worked through each opportunity as it arose. We reframed, relearned, and identified new ways to move forward.

Near the end of our work together, Fisher had been offered a position as a supervisor in his department— something he'd never voiced wanting or being passionate about, but was interested in trying. While he was in the position we talked regularly about frustrations, strategies, and why he wanted to try to make this work—eventually revealing that it wasn't so much the position that he wanted, but the idea that he should take it because it was a logical next step...even though intrinsically it didn't seem to make sense to or for him.

In the last month of our work together, Fisher was asked to step down from the supervisor position. His boss had decided that Fisher had many talents, but the supervisor position he was in wasn't making the most use of his creativity. I sent him an email to check in and see how things were going and how he was navigating the situation.

What I received back made my heart soar: "I feel like the work we did together was crucial to me understanding what was right for me. The demotion? I could call it a failure, but I'm really proud of it. Most of the times I've failed in my life have been because I haven't tried, or I haven't followed through. This time I tried, I realized it wasn't a good fit, I failed, got the feedback I needed to change direction, and I'm moving on. I'm so glad that it happened, otherwise I would always have wondered—and now I know. There's something else meant for me, it's just not that."

I could not have been prouder of him in that moment—and more proud of what we were able to accomplish together.

Failure can create feelings of anxiety and not being good enough...but only if you see it that way.

# Chapter 7: Confidence Crisis

*"Don't compare your insides to someone else's outsides"*
*~ Martha Beck*

## Confidence (source/symptom)

This is the old chicken or egg story, as far as I'm concerned, although I believe that Luna Lovegood (J. K. Rowling's beloved character from Harry Potter) may have said it best when she said, "A circle has no beginning."

It's maddeningly true, in many cases: if you're feeling anxious rather than confident, it is much hard to get what you want, but if you can't get what you want, it's very difficult not to feel anxious and to be confident! As far as I'm concerned, confidence is the ability to feel self-assured, with a knowledge and belief about our own abilities and potential success.

Generally speaking, a confidence crisis (the time that all of that goes away) is the time that I get to take clients back through the many tools we've learned together.

My client, Elizabeth, recently came out to the farm for an Equus Coaching™ session. Before she arrived, she'd told me that she really wanted to focus on her communication skills. Equus Coaching™ is excellent for communication training because we have an opportunity to figure out what we actually want to communicate, and then we have yet another opportunity to practice reading another's nonverbal communication, interpreting it, and responding in a nonverbal way that will actually be received and understood by the other (in this case, a horse). Since horses don't speak English (or any verbal language), it's also a practice in how we communicate what we mean, but play with shifting our style and familiar patterns to meet the needs of the receiver.

As Elizabeth entered the round pen with Sebastian, I invited her to get started by communicating to Sebastian what she'd like him to do. All of a sudden, the strong, confident woman that I had been standing with outside of the round pen became a small and insecure soul standing in front of me.

Right away I could sense that Elizabeth's issue wasn't necessarily communication: it was confidence.

"Elizabeth, it looks like you're having a hard time deciding what you'd like to do with Sebastian right now—can you tell me why?" I asked.

"I just don't really know what to ask because I'm not sure if he'll do it," Elizabeth responded. "And," she went on. "If I don't know if it will work, it feels kind of silly to ask for it."

You may have felt this way at some point in your life (that is, if you're a human).

*I'm not sure if I'll get the promotion, so I just won't apply.*

*I'll be heartbroken if I ask her out and she says no— better to avoid it altogether.*

*I deserve a raise, but if my boss tells me no I'll be humiliated, and I don't know if I could handle that.*

*I'd like to join those women for coffee, but what if they don't want me to join them? I think it best to avoid the rejection.*

*I want my husband to...*

*...do the dishes.*

*...fold the laundry.*

*...get his dirty underwear off the floor, damnit!*

*...but if I ask and he ignores me I'll just get even more pissed off...I'll just keep doing it for him, I'm sure one day he'll get the picture.*

Can you see the problem here? These thoughts alone may not cause the anxiety, but the anxiety of wondering, the overwhelming feeling of being stuck—that's what can end up causing the confidence crisis.

Elizabeth is not alone in this struggle—so many of us struggle with the same problem. Our assumption that we may not get what we want causes us to operate from a place of insecurity and anxiousness, making it far more likely that we won't get what we want. Sometimes because, out of fear, we won't ask or speak up, and occasionally because our lack of confidence does, in fact, affect our ability to reliably communicate. And sometimes our lack of confidence actually interferes with our ability to even trust what we know or want—all of which is what Elizabeth was experiencing.

"Elizabeth, I think I'm hearing you say that you can only ask for what you want if you're sure of what the result would be—correct me if I'm wrong?" I asked.

"Well…I guess that is what I'm saying, but when you say it, it doesn't sound quite right," she laughed.

"What if it were true that, no matter what Sebastian does, *you cannot get this wrong*," I offered. "What if you could try anything—anything at all—and no matter what, it's better than trying nothing? What if the result isn't what matters, but your willingness to ask?"

114

"Oh boy...well...that would feel really...freeing!" Elizabeth said. "So...even if he just stands there and doesn't move, no matter what I do, it's fine?"

I laughed, loving this dialogue. "Elizabeth, if you don't ask, he's still just going to be standing there, not moving...so what have you got to lose?"

"Oh my gosh!" she exclaimed. "That's so funny— but now I see your point! If I ask I may or may not get what I want, but I definitely won't get what I want if I don't ask!"

"Exactly!" I responded.

Over the course of the next hour or so, Elizabeth focused on getting Sebastian to trot in a circle, counter-clockwise.

Not only was she able to get that result several times, but more importantly, she was able to make several surprising discoveries:

First, Elizabeth discovered that before she could ask for anything, she had to know what she was asking for. By identifying and then stating an intention, Elizabeth was able to give clarity to the goal and make it easier to achieve.

Next, she discovered that the more stressed and anxious she got (about what the horse was going to do), and the more attached to the outcome (instead of the journey) the less clear her communication to Sebastian, and the less likely she was to get the result she was looking for. Alternately, the more willing to play with different approaches Elizabeth was, and the more fun she had, the more likely she was to get her desired result: Sebastian at a trot…*so the less she cared if it didn't work out exactly as she hoped, the more likely it was to work!*

Throughout our day together, I had the opportunity to teach Elizabeth various tools to use when she noticed her confidence waning because the reality is that a dip in confidence is typically tied to some kind of stress, anxiety, or overwhelm that is commanding our attention.

As an example, when I first noticed Elizabeth struggle to decide how to spend her time in the round pen, it became apparent that she simply didn't want to "force her decision" upon Sebastian. This was such an excellent opportunity to talk about boundaries: what you do is what you do, what I do is what I do—I'm free to choose, and you're free to choose. Remember? "My business, your business, God's business?" And honestly, there are few greater teachers of this than a fifteen-hundred-pound horse that she actually can't "force" or manipulate to do anything! It was also an opportune time to introduce the body compass to Elizabeth: what did she notice? The pressure and stress when she felt she had to make the "right decision" for everyone, versus the lightness and freedom to simply make a choice that felt right to her. In Elizabeth's case less pressure = more freedom = better result.

As soon as Elizabeth realized that she could decide what she wanted, try different ways of asking, and celebrate small victories, she was willing to take movement. One step clockwise? Awesome! Six steps in a walk counter-clockwise? Even better! Once Elizabeth saw that she could achieve one step, the possibility of achieving two seemed far more doable. You know what they say, you can't steer a parked car! The same is true of horses, and anything else in life. In a real-time experiment, Elizabeth was able to ask for what she wanted, receive feedback, try again, and repeat. She felt what it was like to practice baby steps and celebrate small victories on her way to even bigger ones. Ultimately? She reduced the anxiety that was living within her, and step by step began to develop her confidence muscle.

If you ask for a $1,000 per month raise, and you get $100 per month? Victory! It's more than what you had, and—bonus!—now you know you can ask.

You want your kid to put away his laundry, and he stuffs it into his drawers without folding it? At least you're not the one putting it away! Win!

Maybe you ask an employee to develop a marketing plan, only to find they don't know how…an

117

opportunity to figure out what they need and how to provide them with as little information as possible, but as much as necessary, so that they can embrace their own small victories and develop their confidence (and your marketing plan!) along the way!

You see? Tiny baby steps, celebrate small victories, build on momentum with more momentum…easier said than done, I know…but doable, all the same.

Elizabeth and I discovered that her confidence was also being diluted by her fear of judgement. We worked through that fear with the Thought Work tool (*Elizabeth, is it true that I'm judging you to be a failure?*). We tackled her tendency toward perfectionism and fear of failure by using permissions (*Elizabeth, can you give yourself permission to let this be a little messy and take a little bit more time to figure out?*).

Throughout our day together, Elizabeth and I worked with so many tools that you'd think we were carpenters…with each tool we practiced Elizabeth dramatically increased her self-awareness, while she learned to live with her anxiety. With each baby step, she started feeling less anxious and more confident. From that more confident place, she found herself living more freely and achieving more and more of her desired results. She realized that it was through trying and failing and trying again that she became confident enough to get what she wanted…but that getting what she wanted wasn't the most important achievement of the day. As they so often say, "it's not the destination, but the journey." And so it is with confidence development and anxiety reduction—the lesson that actually ended up being the most important achievement of the day.

Elizabeth is the type of client who I love to work with: smart, capable, accomplished, and struggling to manage the stress, anxiety, and overwhelm that were ultimately keeping her from feeling confident and fully thriving—not only in her career, but in her life. For me, for Elizabeth, and for many of my other clients, we simply need to learn how to build our confidence muscle, sometimes again and again, so that it can serve us when we need it most.

# Chapter 8: But What If...

## "What If" Syndrome (source)

I will never forget my very first paying client. She hired me when I was still working full-time, and I believed that I really had no idea how to be a coach. I remember her saying to me that she felt nervous, overwhelmed, anxious, and stuck, and that she wasn't quite sure why or what to do. I could relate. The words were flying out of my mouth before I could stop them: "I understand. I think I can help you."

Her name was Evie—she was a few years older than me, with kids far older than mine and a career that was very similar as far as the type and volume of responsibility and pressure. She made a good living but was the sole breadwinner in her home, and as such she was very cautious with her investment decisions. She looked at me for a minute—I could tell she was hesitant, and maybe even a bit skeptical—but I could also tell that she was desperate to feel differently, somehow.

"Yes. Okay. I want to try coaching," she said. From there, our stories unfolded together.

The more I got to know Evie, the more intrigued I became. From an outside perspective she was calm, cool, and collected. Virtually unshakeable. She had a knowing smile, her voice was soft and calm, and she never seemed flustered. She excelled at work, and from what I could tell she had an excellent reputation, both personally and professionally. Underneath, however, were insecurities and anxieties that ran so deep and untouched that it was startling, even at times, to her.

I saw so much of myself in Evie.

At the outset of our work together, Evie felt stagnant, which she attributed to her work and she thought she might want to pursue a different career (though she loved the company she worked for.) As time went by, however, what we discovered was that she really just felt anxious and stuck…in general. She was afraid to pursue new hobbies, for fear that she wouldn't be good at them. She was intimidated by the idea of going back to school, because she thought there was a possibility that she would fail. On almost every call, and often between calls, she would reference the deep and anxiety provoking idea that, at any moment, she could be fired from her job for seemingly small mistakes or perceived underperformance.

During our fourth session, Evie told me that her friends had been begging her to try a new clogging class in the town where she lived, but that she wasn't really interested in going. In her voice I heard something that caused me to be unconvinced and curious. Because we'd been talking over several weeks about her tendency to avoid new things, I suspected this was the same pattern in a new, and perfectly coachable, scenario.

"Why aren't you going to the clogging class with your friends?" I inquired, not letting her move onto the next item on her agenda just yet.

Evie was what I like to call a thinker—always needing plenty of space for reflection to be sure that what she would say next was what she meant to say (probably another side effect of not wanting to be misunderstood, misjudged, or wrong). After a measurable silence, she finally answered, "I just don't want people to look at me. What if they look my way and think 'Why's the fat girl here?', or 'Who does she think she is waltzing in here to try this, she's so uncoordinated!' Honestly, I don't even know what they'd be thinking, but I'm sure they'd all be looking at me and thinking I shouldn't be there…so I just won't go."

I could tell that Evie thought that was the end of the discussion. Surprise!

"Evie, do you notice this pattern coming up in other places in your life?" I asked, wondering if she would know what I was referring to.

"Do you mean the pattern of not doing things because I don't want to know what people are thinking about me?" Evie asked astutely.

"Something along those lines. Specifically, I'm wondering how often it comes up that there's something that intrigues you or that you might want to pursue, but you give up on it before you even begin because you're trying to avoid an imagined outcome. A 'what if' moment?"

"Oh that…well…yeah…I do it all the time."

From there, it didn't take much of a leap for Evie to catalogue the various things in life she'd been avoiding for so long: interesting jobs left unapplied for; books unwritten; vacations untaken; hobbies unpursued; adventures untraveled; friendships undeveloped.

The list was long, and, to be honest, a bit heart-wrenching—for both of us. These long unspoken dreams had left Evie feeling not only disappointed, but trapped in a life that felt, in her own words, stagnant, boring, and anything but free.

As her coach, however, I knew that in order to unravel and start again, we had to start small. The list was long, but I had a sense we would come back to this same situation from time to time, because, as I've said before, we notice…then we practice (with lots of self-compassion…which can be hard for us perfectionist, people-pleasing anxious types)…then we master. And sometimes it takes an awful lot of practice.

From the list that Evie had laid out in front of me, I knew that this clogging class was seemingly innocuous, and therefore the perfect place to start to unravel this pattern. The pattern of avoidance because "what if…"

First, I wanted to bring Evie's attention to her body and her body compass.

"So Evie, when you're believing that if you try this clogging class that people will believe that you're foolish, you mentioned that it feels awful. What precisely is happening physically for you right now as you think 'what if people think I'm a fool if I go clogging?'"

"I feel sick to my stomach—just super anxious and tense. I'm, like…grimacing. And my shoulders are hunched, my fists are clenched, and my throat is, like…closing up. I feel really, really anxious and tense. Yuck. That's why I'm not going."

"Because you're anticipating that people will think you're a fool?" I asked.

"Yes—I mean…I don't think it, I just know they'll think that. I can only imagine," Evie told me, firmly committed to her belief.

"When is this clogging class?" I asked, wanting to point something out to Evie.

"Next Thursday," Evie tells me (it's a Friday).

"Do you find it interesting that something that's happening seven days in the future that you are only imagining right now is causing you to feel physically ill?" I asked Evie, curious. "Hmmm…" Evie pondered. "Not really…what if it *is* awful? The idea of it is what makes me sick to my stomach."

It was at that point that I decided to talk about the concept of presence, or as Eckhart Tolle puts it, "The Power of Now." While it's most certainly not true in every scenario, what I have discovered with most of my clients are that the things that are causing them the most stress are things that are either long-gone, or may never actually happen. I call this 'what-if' syndrome:

What if I get fired?

What if my son grows up to be a dickhead?

What if everyone laughs at me?

What if I did that wrong and it comes back to bite me in the ass?

What if I get fired and we have to live on the street?

What if it means that I'm a horrible person that I turned down my brother-in-law's invite?

What if I never get invited anywhere again because I told my friends I was too tired to go out last night?

You get the gist.

I mean…sometimes these things are real possibilities (which still doesn't mean we "know" they will happen). Often they're worse-case scenarios…and sometimes they're just plain outlandish. But that doesn't stop our minds from spinning out into the uncontrollable future, to create stress, avoidance, anxiety, and pure imprisonment.

"Evie, I know the clogging class is next Thursday, and we're going to come back to that…for right now though, I'd like to ask you to just get really present with me for the moment. Go ahead and close your eyes, and get really comfortable. How are you feeling?" I asked.

"I'm good. I'm sitting in my chair at work, and my door is locked so no one can come in," she giggled. "And I feel pretty relaxed."

"Great. I just simply want you to take three, nice, deep belly breaths right now. I'd like you to just slow everything down, so take a nice deep breath in, hold it for three to five seconds, and then let it out very slowly. On the first breath, I want you to let go of everything up to this point. On breath two, I want you to simply arrive and be in this moment…right here, right now. And on breath three, open yourself up to the possibility of what is ahead with an open heart."

As Evie did the "3 Deep Breaths" exercise with me, she became very calm. The pace at which she was speaking slowed down, the frenetic energy in her voice slowed way down, and she just generally became more relaxed.

Breathing seems so simple and cliché—I know. How many times have we heard it: "Just breathe!" Scientifically, however, the reality is that taking a nice slow breath stimulates our vagus nerve, which slows down our heart rates and activates our parasympathetic nervous system…which reduces stress (by taking us out of fight or flight) and helps us to become more present. Science, y'all! Taking a deep breath (and especially three or more) also simply allows us to slow the fuck down. We can check in and remind ourselves that right now, in this current and actual moment, we are okay.

It's taken me years to get the hang of remembering to breathe—slowly and deeply, that is. Occasionally, my husband still looks at me and asks if I'm hyperventilating—at which point I get all worked up and yell at him that I'm taking my three deep breaths and not to watch me!

In any case, as I worked with Evie on the art of presence, she was able to slow down, and check in to remind herself that she was okay, and, at that moment, safe. It was an opportunity for her to remember that on that day, at that moment, she was in her office with a locked door, and no one was laughing at her, pointing at her, or thinking she was a fool.

From that point, Evie and I were able to proceed with the coaching session—because we had let go of the what-ifs and were simply working off what we knew to be true in that moment.

By the end of our session, we had done a full thought work session on her plan to avoid the clogging class, we had checked in with her body compass, and we had practiced the art of staying present.

What Evie discovered? That she would be okay, absolutely okay, if she went to that clogging class. That she wouldn't know how people would respond until she got there, and if she didn't go she would never know. And if she never knew, she would continue to make up what she thought they were going to do—and

Evie's realization? That she was probably making people out to be a lot less patient, and more judgmental, than they would actually be in the moment. And ultimately, that maybe what other people think about her isn't all that important anyway…because what she believes about herself is the only thing that actually matters.

As Evie and I wrapped up her session, we started talking about the idea that living out of presence—in other words, anticipating the worst that might happen, or shuddering over what's already done—might be what was ultimately keeping her stuck.

"Evie," I said gently. "You said that you feel stuck in career, stuck in hobbies, anxious about trying new things… I'm so proud of you for being willing to try this clogging class. Because what we're really talking about is freedom. Freedom to try things. Freedom to choose. Freedom to be imperfect. Freedom to be silly. *Freedom to be foolish*, if that's what it takes. Freedom from the fear, and freedom from the "what ifs" that linger in your head. So the more we can start to wiggle these ideas—'I have to be perfect,' 'I have to do it exactly right the first time,' 'I don't want people to judge me,' 'I can't fail,' 'I have to make everyone happy,' 'I don't know what I want'—the more we can start to shed those fabricated burdens, the more confident you will start to feel, and the more freedom you will have to create the life you've been craving.

For right now, though? Let's just start with this clogging class, because that's what's right in front of us. That is what is now. How does that sound?"

And of course, Evie agreed, because who doesn't want to feel free and unstuck?

Over the course of the next several months that Evie and I worked together, we came back often to focusing simply on what was present.

Together, we practiced the art of the "3 deep breaths." Whenever Evie found herself spinning about what she didn't know but was anxiously anticipating, we came back to "3 deep breaths." In fact, this particular tool came in quite handy, several months down the line, when Evie called me from the state fair....where she was performing in a clogging exhibition! Can you imagine? What freedom, to go from wondering "what if they all laugh at me" to dancing onstage in front of hundreds of people with confidence.

Though Evie continued to live, as we all do, with her uninvited guests (stress, anxiety, and overwhelm), she had learned how to live with them more easily. And as she did, Evie had started to embrace life as her uniquely imperfect self...and along the way, she realized that what she was looking for all along was a peaceful existence, the ability to navigate life *with* her "guests," and, most importantly? Freedom. Freedom to pursue whatever it was that she decided she wanted. Evie later sent me one of the best texts I had ever received—in it, she said:

"I just skipped through Walmart, blowing a pinwheel and giggling, with my sixteen-year-old son. I think he thought I was crazy. I felt crazy. But then we collapsed in an aisle and laughed and laughed. I would never have done that before—I would have been too embarrassed, wondering 'what if they all think I'm crazy?' and I would have missed that memory. But now? I feel free."

And my wish for you is the same: Freedom, to be who you are, do what you dream, live what you love.

*"Twenty years from now you will be more disappointed by the things that you did not do than by the ones you did. So throw off the bowlines. Sail away from the safe harbor. Catch the trade winds in your sails. Explore. Dream. Discover."*

- *Mark Twain (and Samuel Clemens)*

# Conclusion

*"Hatred paralyzes life; love releases it. Hatred confuses life; love harmonizes it. Hatred darkens life; love illuminates it."*
*~ Martin Luther King, Jr.*

## Living with Your Uninvited Guests

Since you're still here, it's time for the spoiler alert: just reading this book won't magically cure your anxiety, your overwhelm or overwhelm paralysis, your nagging worry, your tendency toward perfectionism, or your inability to know what you want, and say what you feel. My intention with this book was to do three things:

1) Help you realize that you are absolutely not alone in your struggles.
2) Introduce tools and concepts that you can use in your daily life to navigate with more freedom from anxiety.
3) Share with you that my support and help is available if and when you're ready for it.

My own anxiety (incessant and uncompromising worry, manifesting in Trichotillomania and OCD)

133

was, at least in part, passed on to me by my dear ol' dad, gifted to him by my sweet grandma Velma, and so on. I think I turned out okay (with plenty of help and support along the way).

I vividly remember being in my junior year of college: I was supposed to be leaving to live and study abroad in Italy for a term with one of my best friends. The timing, however, was miserable. The day of my departure, my mom lay in a hospital bed with not a hair on her head following chemo and radiation, recovering from a second bone marrow transplant that came with her second cancer diagnosis.

My dad had to drive me to the airport, and the entire way I sobbed, which is perfectly normal, I know. I called my mom in her hospital room from the airport payphone, telling her I was changing my mind. I couldn't go. What if she died while I was gone, and I was off gallivanting in Italy? Nope—I couldn't do it. "Change of plans!" I declared with red-rimmed eyes. My dad didn't know what to do with me—he stood off to the side, looking somewhat uncomfortable (honestly, probably kind of agreeing with my plan...since he's the worrier). My mom counter-challenged, and told me in no uncertain terms that I was to get my ass on that plane and go live in Italy— because when else would I get to do that? How was my being here supposed to prevent her from dying- what did I think I was going to do about that, if it were to happen? "Nope!" my mom told me—"You're going, and that's final. If something changes, and I'm going to die, we'll get ahold of you, and you can come home then, but for right now, I'm alive and in the safest place I can possibly be. Call me next Sunday—love you, have a good flight."

Well...that was that. She had laid down the law, and I didn't really feel like I had a choice in the matter—I was getting on that plane and moving to another country. Did her decisive direction stop me from worrying? Oh, no...not at all. In fact, I got on that plane, put my head in my hands, and sobbed for another two hours. My sweet friend Jen sat next to me, holding my hand and rubbing my back the entire time, while I hyperventilated and let my mind do its thing and create a dozen and a half different catastrophes. About halfway across the Atlantic I realized there was no turning back, and I decided to follow my mom's instructions and embrace the situation. I chose to live, alongside my anxiety and worry over what might happen an ocean away. I planned to find a payphone every Sunday to call and check in (I'm dating myself, I know, but cell phones weren't common at the time, adding a bit more uncertainty to the situation), ensure I had a regular planned mail pickup, and that my parents knew my plans and where I would be for the upcoming week. I kept worrying, but I stopped hyperventilating. I was definitely distracted from time to time by the "what-ifs," but I became better and better about not dwelling there for too long.

Plenty of things happened while I was gone (that I didn't plan on and could never have imagined)...but my mom lived. She went home from the hospital, she got stronger, she picked me up from the airport that December and told me that I smelled and needed desperately to take a shower. I've never been so happy to see someone.

That fall was the first time that I really had to learn to live with my uninvited guests, or "frenemies" (stress, worry, anxiety) and not let them absolutely take control of me. I had a lot more practice from there, and it wasn't until I learned the tools in this book that I really started to learn how to respond to how my brain functions with love, and not with hatred, retaliation, and shame.

Maybe you resonate with my story or my son's. Your worry and anxiety come out in unexpected, and sometimes inexplicable, ways—habits, tics, or disorders that don't look like anxiety but are driven out of it. An inability to respond to texts. A nervous habit. A desire to hide.

Perhaps you're more like my daughter. The nervousness you feel in new or unanticipated situations takes you to the point of physical illness, and you find yourself sick in the bathroom before a big presentation.

I bet that, like Zoe or Barrett, you sometimes feel like other people are judging your best effort to be not quite good enough, and it makes you feel crazy and "broken."

Maybe you see yourself in Nora's story (download the bonus chapter now!) or Evie's: smart, capable, accomplished, and yet still insecure and second-guessing your every move to the point that you are sometimes afraid to even take a step for fear it could be in the wrong direction.

Or can you relate to Michelle in some way? Her desire to be the very best, do the very most, and that sometimes you wear yourself out in the process, but you just aren't quite sure what to give up, and don't want anyone—ever—to think that you can't just do it all.

Maybe, like Fisher, you're terrified to fail, you've been avoiding it at all costs, and you feel stuck and unsatisfied—in your career, your business, your life—or in all of it.

But check it out: Zoe and Steven now work together all the time—she's thriving in her recent promotion and is starting to relate to her coworkers in a more relaxed and meaningful way.

Barrett fixed the AC unit. He also accepted an offer for a newly created position within his department, is relearning how to have a healthier relationship with his family of origin, and takes teeny, tiny, continuous action on every work project he's given.

Michelle accepted the position she was offered at work, encompassing her passion for wellness with her desire for financial, dare I say, domination. She all but dropped MLM, and has a full hour or more to do what she wants to with every day.

Fisher is thriving now that he doesn't have to supervise anyone—he survived the failure and took it as feedback that that is not the kind of career he wants. He's now in charge of the department newsletter and deploying hilarious communication throughout the company.

Nora is still figuring out what kind of leader she wants to be—but all the while she's thriving in a leadership position that was literally designed with her in mind.

Evie hasn't yet gone skydiving, but she did perform at that clogging exhibition, she's accepted some special projects at work that interest her, she recently traveled to New Orleans with a friend, and she's loving life. Oh—and she was published! Boom!

Elizabeth and I are continuing to work together on how to communicate from a place of confidence and asking for what she wants. It's a process, but I know she'll get there.

Sandra decided to make a permanent change of direction and quit her stress-filled job to find something that she enjoyed more.

Here's the real secret—it's why I've written this book:

If you've been telling yourself that *suffering through life* with stress, anxiety, overwhelm, or over-commitment is inevitable, I wrote this book for you. Because it's true: life could be so much easier if only you didn't have these uninvited guests at your table…

*And it's also true that even while you're hosting them, life can be sweet.*

Learning to live with the things that are holding you back will only move you forward. It won't be easy, but it can be done, and it can change the way you feel about life and the way you live.

I know. I've been there. I walk the walk every day, and I'm here to tell you that you can do it, too.

# Thank You

Thank you for reading!

If you have thoughts, questions, or would like to discuss how to get some ongoing and individualized support, please email me at meagan@meaganenglishcoaching.com

or you can comment or follow me on Facebook at https://www.facebook.com/meaganenglishcoaching

**BONUS CHAPTER**

For your free "Bonus Chapter" make sure to visit:
www.meaganenglishcoaching.com/uninvitedguest/bonus

**FREE TOOLS**

To access your free tools, worksheets and companion to "Uninvited Guest" visit:
www.meaganenglishcoaching.com/uninvitedguest/tools

**WANT MORE ONGOING SUPPORT?**

It's my goal that those of you that feel capable and compelled to do so, can move forward and start using the tools, exercises and concepts contained in this book to make transformations in how you live independently, should you choose to do so.

For those of you that want ongoing support, however, there are various options:

## GROUP PROGRAMS

In these virtual group programs, I teach concepts from the book live to a limited group of participants over a pre-defined period. Every call includes learning a new concept, discussion and Q&A, and an opportunity to be coached by me, in a group setting on whatever we're learning about (or anything else!)

There's something really powerful about learning in a safe and contained space, alongside others that know you're struggle—even if it's not exactly the same—and being supported while being in the comfort of your own space. The camaraderie, the support, and the community are a gift in and of themselves. Find out more about going to www.meaganenglishcoaching.com/programs-live-events/ and setting up a strategy session.

## LIVE EQUUS EVENTS

I'm not kidding when I tell you that going to my first Equus Coaching™ Workshop literally changed my life. I arrived to the workshop thinking, "What the hell is this voodoo", and I left thinking, "Holy shit I have to learn how to do this and share it with the world."

To find out more about upcoming Live Equus Events for small groups where you can learn the concepts within this book in a intensive and incredible environment, with both horse and human at your side, email me or go to www.meaganenglishcoaching.com/equus-coaching/ to sign up for notifications, and see what's coming up!

# PRIVATE ONE-ON-ONE COACHING

It was through Private Coaching that I really made long-term life transformations, including how to change my thinking, how to take risks, and how to live—freely and fully—with all of the things that life has to offer (including those pesky uninvited guests).

As a Coach I serve as an objective and totally non-judgmental listening partner, a strategist, a perspective-giver, a sometimes-teacher (and always-learner), and a support and motivation system—just for you. I care about you, I will hold you accountable, but I am not invested in what you think, what you say, or what you do. Where else do you really get that? But I believe that's yours to own. I serve as a compassionate witness to your decisions and experience, while walking the journey with you as you learn and grow. I work with most of my clients virtually in ongoing one-on-one work (which means I can work with anyone, anywhere), and grow to love each and every client that I serve. I take a limited number of one-on-one clients at a time, so that I can focus and best serve each of you. If you're interested in a more individualized and private experience, I'd love to offer you a complimentary and confidential strategy session. Let's figure out what's holding you back, and then get you where you want to go.

Set up a strategy session by visiting
www.meaganenglishcoaching.com and click "Get
Started Now" or email me at
meagan@meaganenglishcoaching.com

# Further Reading

*Daring Greatly* by Brené Brown

*Loving What Is* by Byron Katie

*Finding Your Own North Star* by Martha Beck

*Search Inside Yourself* by Chade-Meng Tan

*The Gifts of Imperfection* by Brené Brown

*Big Magic* by Elizabeth Gilbert

*Steering by Starlight* by Martha Beck

# Acknowledgments

I've always wanted to write a book…I just always thought that my first book would be a coffee-book compilation of hilarious kid-quotes (since that's what most of my life is spent navigating). I always somehow managed to avoid finding the time, inspiration or motivation to get it done, however. The first summer after leaving my corporate job and being deep into my coaching practice, the idea for this book formed. I had spent nearly two years, at that point, helping clients find freedom from self-judgement, anxiety, stress, and start living their lives fully, with joy and freedom, and I was inspired daily. One seemingly innocuous day in June, I received an email announcing an opportunity to write a book with a woman that inspired me greatly: Angela Lauria of "The Author Incubator"—as the name implies, she grows authors, and she certainly incubated me! (https://theauthorincubator.com/). Without my dear clients and their brave journeys, Angela and her frank feedback and continuous motivation, and the support of my family, this book may never have come to life.

To each and every one of my clients that has trusted me, inspired me, and allowed me a glimpse into their lives and their journeys: You know who you are, and I hope you know how much your bravery and desire to live more fully moves me to live mine. I can't believe how lucky I am to work with every single one of you that crosses my path—by whatever design that takes.

To my mentors—the women that created and challenged me as a Coach and cultivated the Tribe and Herd that I have grown to love so dearly: Martha Beck (http://marthabeckinstitute.com/), Koelle Simpson and Angela Lauria: Your guidance, feedback, nurturing and true passion for developing others is a gift to me, and to the world.

A huge shout out to Koelle Simpson, founder of the Koelle Institute for Equus Coaching (https://koellcinstitute.com/): Thank you, thank you, thank you—not only for writing my foreword, and for your unwavering and generous support and love, but for creating Equus Coaching™. It is the work that taught me how to play, how to find joy, and how to start learning to live with my own uninvited guests. I've never been so proud and so humbled as I am to be a provider of this work in the world.

To the most incredible book team a woman could ask for:

My undying gratitude to Cameron Hill (www.TheinhabitedLife.com)—You are an incredible Editor, Photographer and Coach...but more than that, you are a friend, confidante, partner and ally—without you, this book would feel incomplete. Thank you for your creative spirit and generosity.

A huge thank you to Ally Nathaniel of e-Book Publishing Services (http://www.allynathaniel.com/) for helping me navigate the boutique publishing world, and helping me bring this book to life, so that it can serve the people that need it most.

To my fantastic and devoted book launch team: Aaron English, Alex Lewis, Alicia Thompson, Alisa Clark, Amy Hanlon Newell, Angelica Williams, Angi Dilkes Perry, Angie Fogg, Becky Fortier, Brandi Ebner, Bruce Crowell, Carolyn Norman, Cassandra Drumm, Christine Prather, Cristina Forney, Crystal Elder, Daniel Canchola, Darcie Galusha, Debbie Newport, Gina Hosford, Gloria Montes, Heather French, Holly Johnson, Jamie Wyland, Jen Humcke, Jill Hill, Katie Engerman, Kristi VanVleck, Kristi Morgan, Kylie Evenhus, Kym Wells, Lesley Carvalho, Linda Riedman, Luanne Durdan, Matt Barnhart, McKenzie Dodge, Megan Konold, Melodie King, Nancy Guerrera, Nick Lukens, Nicole Croizier, Pat Fisher, Sierra Acker, Suesan Thompson, Susie Osborn, Tara Manske, Tara Polich, Thomasina Nugent and Tracy Hovanic. Thank you for reading, caring about, reviewing, and sharing my work—I am blessed to have each and every one of you in my corner.

To my friends, my supporters, my clients, my tribe, my herd: Thank you for your company along the journey. For your cheers from both near and far. For your belief in me that I could do things that I wasn't sure were possible. I have lots of love for you, my peeps.

To my family: Mom and Dad, your belief in me never waivers and I am so grateful. To my brothers, Paul and Joe, and their families: Thank you for teaching me how to be tough, brave, and a defender of others. You have always helped me find humor in every situation. To my in-laws, grandparents, cousins, nieces and nephews: You all rock. And are my rocks. Love to you every single one of you listed here.

Finally, the most gargantuan gratitude in all of the world is reserved for my family: My children Landon and Gracie, and my supportive and patient husband Aaron. You are all my inspiration—always and every day. Watching you brave the world, live fully and love others. None of this would mean anything if I couldn't share it with you. Thank you for loving me, in all my craziness, in every loud moment, and every bear hug. You're the best things about my life—always.

# About the Author

Meagan English is a Certified Life and Equus Coach™, as well as an author, speaker, and consultant. Meagan specializes in helping professional men and women to discover what they want most, what's standing in their way, and then supports them in breaking through those obstacles to achieve their very best—in both their life, and career (primarily via one-on-one coaching and small virtual groups). Prior to starting her coaching practice, Meagan spent the previous fifteen years of her career in business operations and leadership development, ultimately overseeing multi-million dollar business units, and many hundreds of staff. Over the course of her career, Meagan created leadership training programs and supported countless mentees in their leadership and career development. As a wife, mother and now-entrepreneur she understands the complicated dynamics of balancing passion, purpose and responsibility to create a well-lived life, and she is endlessly motivated to help others do the same.

Meagan holds a degree from Oregon State University and holds Coaching Certifications through the Martha Beck Institute™ and the Koelle Institute for Equus Coaching™. Meagan has served on various volunteer Boards of Directors, and is a Company Advisor for Young Entrepreneurs Business Week. In 2010 she was honored to receive the "President's Award of Merit". Meagan travels throughout the NW and beyond to speak at conferences, and consults with several corporations relative to team and individual leadership development.

Meagan lives near Portland, OR and loves hosting backyard BBQ's, hanging out with family and friends, playing with ponies at the farm, and volunteering to coach youth sports (while she cheers her kids on!)

**Website:** www.meaganenglishcoaching.com

**Email:** meagan@meaganenglishcoaching.com

**Facebook:**
https://www.facebook.com/MeaganEnglishCoaching/

**LinkedIn:**
https://www.linkedin.com/in/meaganenglishcoaching

44884648R00095

Made in the USA
San Bernardino, CA
25 January 2017